To Be Clear

*Proclaiming the Gospel
in a Post-Truth World*

By Dr. Walter Swaim

Critical Mass Books
Davenport, Florida
www.criticalmasspublishing.com

Cover Design   Eowyn Riggins
Interior Layout   Rachel Greene

ISBN: 978-1-947153-20-2

Contents

Acknowledgments

It has been said that much of who we are is a sum of all those who impacted our lives along the way.

I am careful to give honor and glory first to my Lord and Savior, Jesus Christ. He pulled me out of the miry clay and set my feet on solid ground. If not for Him, I would be lost at sea, without regard for life or eternity.

I am forever grateful to my wife, Denise, who patiently endured my long hours working on this and previous educational goals. She has been my biggest fan, friend, lover and the greatest woman a man could ever call his wife. She is my gift from God.

I am immensely thankful for all of my children, now grown adults, as they cheered me on and encouraged me to take this project on, seeing nothing but success at the end.

I am grateful for the godly men in my local church who shaped and molded me for life as a man of God through their example and counsel. Frank Liedkie, Bud McCord, Verle Ackerman, Jim Zabloski, Stan DeVaney, and so many more; space does not allow me to name them here. I am forever indebted to them.

I am also grateful for my Bible college and seminary professors who made an indelible impact on my life for the Lord by training me in the Word. Dr. Hunter Sherman, Dr. Doug Kutilek, Dr. Wofford, Sandy Huntsman, Bill Dowell, Jr. They were the glue that kept my mind and heart together for Christ. Dr. Sherman, in particular, has been not only my professor of professors, but also a friend and the one who urged me to take this step and continue even further. Lastly, I am grateful to Darwin Pennye who urged me to take the steps of completing my M.Div. and doctorate. To all of these, I am grateful beyond words.

Thank you, everyone.

Chapter 1

Introduction

"I reject your facts."

These words were abruptly uttered by House Speaker Nancy Pelosi in a January 4, 2019 meeting with President Trump and Homeland Security Secretary Kirstjen Nielsen. During the government shutdown, an impasse occurred between the White House and the new Congressional leaders. In this meeting, Nielsen was sharing the empirical data and statistics related to the border crisis. According to the Wall Street Journal the tense exchange unfolded at this moment: "I reject your facts," Ms. Pelosi said. "These aren't my facts," Ms. Nielsen claimed. "These are the facts."[1]

This exchange perhaps best encapsulates the dilemma we find ourselves in within our Western culture today. The dilemma is called *post-truth*, and it permeates everything, not just politics. It is here to stay as the new reality of thinking, language, and behavior.

This book will examine the surging post-truth dilemma, particularly in American culture, tracing its historical origin and pervasiveness today in numerous critical areas, such as morality, politics, education, science, and more.

Lastly, we will examine the challenges the church faces to its fundamental doctrine, and, of most concern, to the Gospel message and mission worldwide. Finally, we will see how truth – especially that of Jesus and the Gospel – will be victorious.

1. Rebecca Ballhaus, Alex Leary, and Michael C. Bender, "Trump Considers Declaring National Emergency to Build Border Wall," Politics, Wall Street Journal, January 4, 2019, accessed December 26, 2019, https://www.wsj.com/articles/schumer-pelosi-report-on-progress-on-shutdown-after-talks-with-trump-11546627419.

Chapter 2

A Short History of the Term Post-truth

Though the term, post-truth, is a common fixture in American English vocabulary today, it has a loosely linked history of appearances in the past. Most research has revealed that Serbian-American playwright Steve Tesich first coined the word in a January 1992 article in *The Nation* magazine.[1] His description arises out of political and ethical concerns for the nation. In the wake of the

1. Richard Kreitner, "Consequences: What a 25-Year-Old Essay Tells Us About the Current Moment," Nation, November 30, 2016, accessed January 5, 2019, http://www.thenation.com/article/post-truth-and-its-consequences-what-a-25-year-old-essay-tells-us-about-the-current-moment/.

harshness of the realities of Watergate and Vietnam, he expressed his concern:

> We came to equate truth with bad news and we didn't want bad news anymore, no matter how true or vital to our health as a nation. We looked to our government to protect us from the truth" and that "In a very fundamental way we, as a free people, have freely decided that we want to live in some post-truth world.[2]

The next appearance of the term is found in a book published in 2004 by Ralph Keyes, and it is directly titled, *The Post Truth Era*. His book, written twelve years before the 2016 presidential election that jolted forward the term, post-truth, is a treatise on the wanton dishonesty of Western culture and it has proven to be incredibly prophetic.

Keyes, who saw the term, post-truth, first in Tesich's essay, now sees it with ever widened meaning in our national conscience:

> Post-truthfulness exists in an ethical twilight zone. It allows us to dissemble without considering ourselves dishonest. When our behavior conflicts with our values, what we're most likely to do is reconceive our values. Few of us want to think of ourselves as being unethical, let alone admit that to others, so we devise alternative approaches to morality. Think of them as alt.ethics. This term refers to ethical systems in which dissembling is

2. Steve Tesich, "A Government of Lies," Free Library, January 6, 1992, accessed October 1, 2018, https://www.thefreelibrary.com/A+government+of+lies.-a011665982.

considered okay, not necessarily wrong, therefore not really "dishonest" in the negative sense of the word.[3]

Then finally, out of the raucous 2016 American presidential elections arose the descriptive term, *fake news*. It was popularized by presidential Republican candidate, Donald Trump, referring to the constant manufacture of journalistic news reports whose facts were soon found afterwards to be based on unverified actions and words. This, in turn, engendered the resurgence of the term post-truth.

Fake news has been around for many years, ever since the beginning of the Gutenberg printing press in 1493. However, the new term itself was reborn in 2016 when Oxford Dictionaries officially named the hyphenated word, *post-truth*, as their Word of the Year. It was chosen from a field of many other words growing in popularity at the same time. Its usage that year increased 2,000 times over its use in 2015. Since then, it is ubiquitous in journalistic, political, academic, scientific, philosophical, and religious writing and discussion. In the press release from Oxford Dictionaries, they explain the use of the hyphen in the term post-truth.

> The compound word post-truth exemplifies an expansion in the meaning of the prefix post- that has become increasingly prominent in recent years. Rather than simply referring to the time after a specified situation or event – as in post-war or post-match – the prefix in post-truth has a meaning more like 'belonging to a time in which the specified concept has become

3. Ralph Keyes, *The Post-Truth Era: Dishonesty and Deception in Contemporary Life* New York: St. Martin's Press, 2004), Location 232.

unimportant or irrelevant' Casper Grathwohl, President of Oxford Dictionaries, said, ". . . I wouldn't be surprised if post-truth becomes one of the defining words of our time."[4]

His statement carries more truth in it than realized. The impact of our post-truth world will define not only the culture in general but also define a formidable and slippery challenge to the Gospel's proclamation and presence.

4. Oxford Dictionaries, "Word of the Year 2016 is...," English Oxford Living Dictionaries, accessed August 11, 2018, http://en.oxforddictionaries.com/word-of-the-year/word-of-the-year-2016.

Chapter 3

The Definition of Post-truth

How is post-truth actually defined? For that answer, we return to the Oxford Dictionary, which defines it as "relating to or denoting circumstances in which objective facts are less influential in shaping public opinion than appeals to emotion and personal belief."[1]

In the Cambridge dictionary it is defined as: "relating to a situation in which people are more likely to accept an argument based

---

1. Oxford Dictionaries, "Word of the Year 2016 is...," English Oxford Living Dictionaries, accessed August 14, 2018, http://en.oxforddictionaries.com/word-of-the-year/word-of-the-year-2016.

on their emotions and beliefs, rather than one based on facts."[2] Personal preferences, beliefs and feelings, regardless of the objective reality, are recognized as the culture's final standard for our present post-truth society by many from both liberal and conservative leaders of thought and philosophy.

British journalist Matthew d'Ancona states: "This is the defining characteristic of the Post-Truth world. The point is not to determine the truth by the process of rational evaluation, assessment, and conclusion. You choose your own reality, as if from a buffet. You also select your own falsehood, no less arbitrarily."[3] British philosopher and author, Julian Baggini, buttresses this with the motive he believes created post-truth's reliance on feelings as its arbiter:

> Underpinning this world-weary cynicism is a kind of defeatism, an acceptance that we do not have the resources to discern who's telling the truth and who's just trying it on. Feeling unable to distinguish truth from falsehood, electorates choose their politicians on other, more emotional factors. Losing trust in our brains, we tend to go with our guts and hearts instead.[4]

Unlike the postmodern world, where objective standards of truth are not recognized as any more than human constructs, the

2. *Cambridge Dictionary* s.v., "Post-truth," accessed August 20, 2019,
   https://dictionary.cambridge.org/us/dictionary/english/post-truth.

3. Matthew d'Ancona, *Post Truth: The New War on Truth and How to Fight Back*,
   kindle ed. (London: Ebury Press, 2017), 55.

4. Julian Baggini, *A Short History of Truth*, kindle ed. (London: Quercus Editions
   Ltd, 2017), Location 97.

post-truth world may see specific facts and truth but entirely dismiss them for their own beliefs which they regard as being ultimately true.

Consultant and writer Phil Mobley writes, "A post-truth world, then, is not one in which the truth has ceased to exist; it is one in which it no longer matters."[5] Journalist and now pastor John Dickerson puts it this way: "Western society was once founded on truth, but it has now moved beyond it."[6] Ironically, the subjectively created term post-truth has an objectively established definition that everyone now uses agreeably and uniformly – without regard to personal feelings or preferences.

It also needs to be noted that post-truth has morphed from being used as an adjective (i.e.. in this post-truth culture) to a stand-alone noun. As a noun, it describes a defined state of belief based on preference and feeling, regardless of empirical facts which may prove otherwise.

Interestingly, the term, with the same definition, has already quickly entered other languages in the Western world, particularly the Spanish language. In Spain, where it was also announced as the word of the year for 2017 by the international vanguard of the correct Spanish language, the term is written as *posverdad* (without a hyphen). As in English, the term had previous usage in Spanish

5. Phil Mobley, "Post-truth (And Consequences)," In The World, Online Magazine of the Presbyterian Church of America-byFaith, November 27, 2018, accessed August 20, 2019, https://dictionary.cambridge.org/us/dictionary/english/post-truth.

6. John S. Dickerson, *Hope of Nations: Standing Strong in a Post-truth, Post-Christian World*, kindle ed. (Grand Rapids, Michigan: Zondervan, 2018), 13.

literature and reached a similarly dramatic increase establishing it as a legitimate term for speaking and writing.[7]

Most of the recent literature about post-truth has been focused primarily on the 2016 American presidential election and its political and media-related implications. However, post-truth influence reaches far broader and deeper than those areas, and it is the objective of this book to reveal its inescapable presence in vital areas of our society.

The usage of the term can be more accurately described as not only rejecting objective truth, but also co-opting it by making personal preferences and opinions the objective truth. Post-truth says because a person so profoundly believes that their truth is *the* truth, then it must be forcefully established as such for everyone. World-renowned Christian apologist, Dr. Ravi Zacharias, explains something similar as he explains there are two sides to Post-truth:

> For what it's worth, let's get to the definition of post-truth. There is a soft side to the meaning that suggests that objective facts are less influential in shaping public opinion than are appeals to emotion and personal belief. Well, that is hardly new. But the hard meaning being smuggled in here tells us that in this culture we willfully and justifiably convey something false because it accomplishes a personal or end goal. The end justifies

7. Alex Grijelmo and Heather Galloway, "Post-truth' enters the Spanish dictionary," El Pais, July 5, 2017, accessed October 4, 2018, https://elpais.com/elpais/2017/07/04/inenglish/1499157964_368288.html.

the means and the means, in effect, do not need to justify themselves.[8]

It is mostly observed that post-truth is not a flash-in-the-pan political sound bite or temporary fad in the pop culture language of the day. Post-truth is the basis of the world we live in daily. It is the way reality is perceived and presented now and for the foreseeable future. It is the foundation from which ideas, concepts, philosophies, policies, rules, laws, and behavior are shaped and demonstrated in our modern society. Again, John Dickerson succinctly describes a post-truth society as "a society where a majority of people set their own standards for moral right and wrong, based on their own feelings and regardless of fact."[9] It is the ever-increasing *modus operandi* of our American mentality and behavior in almost everything of importance in which we are engaged.

In the following pages, an analysis will be made of just how insidious post-truth is as a basis and methodology that is rapidly taking control of several of the most prominent and vital fields that guide our societal development and function. We will offer a critique of its consequential damaging effects.

8. Ravi Zacarias, "The Death of Truth and Postmortem," Self-published, RZIM, December 20, 2016, accessed October 1, 2018, http://rzim.org/global-blog/the-death-of-truth-and-a-postmortem/#_ednref1.
9. Dickerson, *Hope of Nations*, 13.

Chapter 4

How Did We Get Here?

In reading a few of the books and articles of today, most would deduce that post-truth has only been a product of the Trumpian political era since 2016. A more careful study reveals that past influences led up to this period, culturally and historically, and caused this drift over many years into an age of deciding and forming axioms based on feelings over facts.

The history of mankind is a long and winding river of fallen thinking and empty approaches to everything around him. Man's continual shifting of thought has always been manifested in the areas of literature, arts, philosophy, science, religion, culture, and more.

This shifting of thought is generally described as three previous, consecutive general phases: Premodernism, Modernism, and Postmodernism. Though there are no clearly defined beginnings or endings to each one, their respective descriptions accurately capture the overlapping transition between the mindset and behavior of each period.

Pre-modernism

From the sixth century until Greece's inclusion within the Roman Empire, we have what is called the *Classical Period* of Greek philosophy. Within this period arose the two most important Greek philosophers, much of whose thoughts and theories influence Western society today.

These Greek teachers attempted, in a non-religious way, to answer the deeper and yet common questions about our existence, purpose, and beginnings. "The various Greek philosophies were essentially religious, providing explanations of the universe and offering salvation through human reason."[1] Though differing in ways and terminology, they still arrived at a general idea of an objective, external, unseen, and unchanging reality that influences us and the world.

In the fifth century B.C., Platonism, in all its various shades of thought itself, was dualistic and described what was called the Twin Pillars:

1. Steve W. Lemke, ""Hellenism," in *Holman Illustrated Bible Dictionary*, ed. Chad Brand (Nashville: Holman Bible Publishers, 2003), 746.

There is an invisible reality that is higher than the physical world, and that human beings understood at the deepest level are also spiritual beings who have a natural affinity to that higher reality. Though the natural and supernatural worlds existed, Plato believed the natural world was really a shadow; the real world was the supernatural world of the soul.[2]

In the fourth century B.C., Aristotle taught his view of God by calling him (or it) the *Unmoved Mover*, that reality that explains all change without changing itself in any way. "This reality is God"[3] and this "unmoved mover causes the cosmos to move toward its own perfection."[4]

From this, the Western world then entered into the Hellenistic Age, which spanned roughly from 300 BC to 300 AD. Hellenism became predominant in this period. Although Greece was conquered militarily by Rome, Greek culture (especially its language) was adopted and permeated the empire. Hellenism is "That unique blend of Greek cultural, philosophical and ethical ideals which after Alexander the Great had a profound effect on the development of culture throughout the Mediterranean world."[5]

2. Lemke, *Holman Illustrated Bible Dictionary*, 746.
3. C. Stephen Evans, *A History of Western Philosophy: From the Pre-Socratics to Postmodernism*, Location 1394 ed. (Downers Grove: InterVarsity Press, 2018), Location 1394.
4. Jacob N. Graham, "Ancient Greek Philosophy," Internet Encyclopedia of Philosophy, accessed December 26, 2019, http://www.iep.utm.edu/greekphi/.
5. Grant R. Osborne, ""Hellenism," in *Baker Encyclopedia of the Bible*, ed. Didier Fassin (Grand Rapids, MI: Baker Book House, 1988), 955.

Once Hellenism became the mainstream culture throughout the Roman Empire, its Greek philosophy "that the physical world represented the temporal, transitory, and evil, while the world of the soul was eternal, real, and good"[6] shaped the intellectual context from which Christianity emerged (though not originated). In its beginnings, and years after, Greek philosophy tore down much of man's polytheistic beliefs and became man's substitute for religious thought. Gradually, though, from its peak in Plato, Greek philosophy became very stratified and watered down.

> At the time of Christ's advent, philosophy had declined from the peak reached by Plato to a system of self-centered individualistic thought such as Stoicism or Epicureanism. Moreover, philosophy could only seek for God and posit Him as an intellectual abstraction; it could never reveal a personal God of love. This bankruptcy of philosophy by the time of the coming of Christ disposed men's minds toward a more spiritual approach to life. Christianity alone was capable of filling the vacuum in the spiritual life of the day.[7]

Greek philosophy had laid open for people the remaining general ideas of the immortality of the soul, an unseen eternal reality, and the need for a justification for how right and wrong is determined. The eventual weakness and downfall created an

6. Lemke, *Holman Illustrated Bible Dictionary*, 746.

7. Earle E. Cairns, *Christianity Through the Centuries: A History of the Christian Church*, 3rd ed. (Grand Rapids: MI: Zondervan, 1996), Location 628. Kindle Edition.

emptiness of answers which Christianity, or Jesus and the Scriptures, were able to fill. The greatest fulfillment of true Christianity did not just satisfy intellectual emptiness but also the emotional and spiritual emptiness through a direct, personal, and loving relationship with the Creator God.

After the tumultuous up-and-down periods of persecution of Christians for many years came the era of freedom for the Christian faith. This was due to the legal status and protection now afforded Christianity by Constantine. As the Christian era arose and further spread her wings from that time onward, the Church then became the unquestioned harbinger and authority of the only divine and objective truths.

The Source for this truth was God as revealed through the Scriptures and propagated and defended by the Church. This ecclesiastical foundation of the pre-modern period became the generally accepted truth and authority, objectively given by God, and was the reason for all things created and discovered. The secular and sacred (including the sciences, art, literature) were one.

> The transition from what is often called the pre-modern period into the modern period corresponds with the influence of Enlightenment thinking and the scientific revolution. Prior to the Enlightenment, there was a dominant cultural belief in the existence of the supernatural. This was due in large part to the rise of Christianity and specifically the Roman Catholic Church as the most powerful cultural presence in medieval times. This was a world of authority, and authority rested in the hands of

traditional institutions, especially the church, since it was entrusted with interpreting and communicating this truth to the common person. With a belief in God came a strong belief in the concept of revelation, that God not only existed but had revealed Himself and His will in the Bible. This revelation was considered the primary source of truth and could be trusted to unlock God's metanarrative (or, Big Story) for the world.[8]

This Christ and church-centered foundation predominated as a network of deeply held and defended abstract principles of belief in the general populous' conscience for centuries. Divine-centered doctrine and philosophy was the filter through which all things were understood and judged in the sciences, art, literature, ethics, and language. D.A. Carson further characterizes the Pre-modern era this way:

> Premodern epistemology is a notoriously loose catchall category for what is common in Judeo-Christian epistemology before the Enlightenment. The important fact is that most people presupposed that God exists and knows everything. That means that all human knowing is necessarily an infinitesimally small subset of God's knowledge. Otherwise put, our knowledge depends on revelation—i.e., on God disclosing some part of what he knows, however that revelation is accomplished. On this point, a great medieval theologian like Thomas Aquinas and a great Reformer like John Calvin were agreed. This means that

8. G. Phillips, W. Brown, and J. Stonestreet, "Theism: The World from God's Hands," in *Making Sense of Your World*, second edition ed. (Salem, WI: Sheffield Publishing Company, 2008), 50.

for the premoderns, epistemology does not begin with the self, with me: it begins with God.[9]

Being unquestioned (at least openly), this centuries-long period of philosophy summarizes what we call today the pre-modern era, which extended into the middle centuries (mid-1600's).

Modernism

From the middle seventeenth century until the mid-twentieth century, the predominant thinking shifted and morphed into what was called Modernism (or the Modern Period) during which the Renaissance and the Enlightenment periods also were concurrent. The Renaissance Period identified the changes in the arts and literature, whereas the Enlightenment was more descriptive of the changes in philosophy during this time.

> The Enlightenment was a movement among European intellectuals in the seventeenth and eighteenth centuries. In the decades leading up to this time, the church's authority had been successfully challenged politically (reactions against corruption), theologically (Luther, Calvin and the Protestant Reformation), philosophically (downfall of scholasticism), and scientifically (Galileo, Copernicus, and Baconian method). There was a growing disillusionment with the traditional educational, political and religious institutions, as well as their authoritative

9. D. A. Carson, *Becoming Conversant with the Emerging Church: Understanding a Movement and Its Implications*, kindle ed. (Grand Rapids, Mich: Zondervan, 2005), 1552.

sources. During the Enlightenment, authority shifted from traditional institutions to human reason. A scientific approach to the world yielded tremendous advances in medicine, technology, and communications and challenged the centrality of theology and religious belief as the paradigm for learning. Free from the restrictive shackles of traditional beliefs (thus, modernism), progress seemed inevitable.[10]

Modernist thinkers began to break away from the centuries-long acceptance of divine revelation-based truth claims, which had been mostly taken for granted for centuries. The answers from the church did not satisfy man's questions any longer and so man's thinking lurched to himself and nature alone as the focus from which all things can be explained.

Modern thinkers start from nature— instead of starting with some form of the supernatural, which had been the characteristic starting point of pre-modern, Medieval philosophy. Modern thinkers stress that perception and reason are the human means of knowing nature in contrast to the pre-modern reliance upon tradition, faith, and mysticism. Modern thinkers stress human autonomy and the human capacity for forming one's own character— in contrast to the pre-modern emphasis upon dependence and original sin. "Modern thinkers emphasize the individual, seeing the individual as the unit of reality, holding that the individual's mind is sovereign, and that the individual is the unit of value— in contrast to the pre-modernist,

10. Phillips, Brown, and Stonestreet, *Making Sense Of*, 50.

feudal subordination of the individual to higher political, social, or religious realities and authorities."[11]

During this period, a monumental shift began to change the relationship between what is called the sacred and the secular. In the pre-modern mind, the sacred explained the secular without any division between the two. The divine gave all answers to the secular. Modernism split the two, and even today, we suffer the consequences of this false dichotomy. For a modernist, their mentality was that "Humans could control the secular, including the natural or physical world because God no longer was doing so."[12]

Modernism quickly became not just a rising, opposing opinion, but a way of thinking and behaving that was quickly penetrating all levels of function in Western society. Dennis McCallum, in his book *The Death of Truth* explains, "Modernists view the world, including humans, as one gigantic machine, placing their faith in rationality (the ability of humans to understand their world), empiricism (the belief that knowledge can only be gained through our senses), and in the application of rationality and empiricism through science and technology."[13]

---

11. Stephen R. C. Hicks, *Explaining Postmodernism*, expanded kindle edition ed. (n.p.: Ockham's Razor Publishing, 2014), Location 584.

12. Stephen M. Feldman, *American Legal Thought From Premodernism to Postmodernism*, Locations 246-247 ed. (New York: Oxford University Press, 2000).

13. Dennis McCallum, ed., *The Death of Truth* (Minneapolis, Minn: Bethany House Publishers, 1996), Location 50.

As a result, man became more confident of his own power, intellect, abilities, and achievements. Secularism was proliferating, and man saw limitless possibilities that could bring solutions to mankind's maladies, bring world peace, and allow mankind to live more comfortable lives. This was due to the continuing technological advances of automation and industry (e.g., the Industrial Revolution, the automobile, the "unsinkable" Titanic) such as humanity had never before known or experienced:

> . . . a modernist self began to emerge, asserting almost Godlike powers to choose values and goals and thus to control and remake the natural and social worlds. Indeed, the various elements of modernism began to crystallize into a coherent worldview: the individual self's ability to reason and to gain foundational knowledge facilitated human control of the secular world and thus engendered endless progress. As modernism moved forward, knowledge increasingly came to be viewed as the means for human liberation in the secular world.[14]

Perhaps the most substantial impact of man-centered thought and emphasis brought to mankind during this period came from Charles Darwin and his book, *The Origins of Species*. This book ushered in the revolutionary theory of Darwinian evolution to the forefront of scientific and popular thinking. He explained that all things came into existence over eons of time through purely random natural means. As the late theologian and author David Breese describes, "The rule, it is said, that obtains in the jungle is that the

14. Feldman, *American Legal Thought From, Location 345.*

strong overcome the weak. The strong, therefore, survive, and the weak become fodder for the strong. With the help of Darwin, this rule was dignified by being called natural selection."[15] This new idea left the question of God's involvement as the Creator and Sustainer open or tabled. Now science would be interpreted through this lens and continues to be so today.

In pre-modernism, God and the Bible were the unquestioned sources of knowledge and practice interpreted and mandated by the Catholic Church. In the modern period, that hierarchy was replaced by science and the university. In modernism, truth was not divinely given but was a set of ideas that man came to know through his rational thinking and *empiricism*. The definition of empiricism is: "… the view that all concepts originate in experience, that all concepts are about or applicable to things that can be experienced, or that all rationally acceptable beliefs or propositions are justifiable or knowable only through experience."[16] More briefly, it is the dependence on and faith in observational and experimental evidence. God and divine revelation would at best be considered distantly uninvolved, or His existence either doubted or entirely negated. "The world of the natural sciences was impressed. It is almost as if the scientists were waiting for such a view."[17] God was rapidly eliminated

15. Dave Breese, *Seven Men Who Rule the World from the Grave* (Chicago: Moody Press, 1990), 31.
16. Brian Duignan et al., "Empiricism," Encyclopædia Britannica, July 22, 2016, accessed December 26, 2019, https://www.britannica.com/topic/empiricism.
17. Breese, *Seven Men Who Rule*, 30.

from the exploration, study, and discoveries of the world by scientists and laypeople alike:

> Modernism was the belief that reason had the power to make sense out of the world; the human mind, it was thought, has the ability to interpret reality and discover overarching values. It was optimistic, believing in progress; there was the belief that science and history could lead us to various truths that would help us interpret reality. Modernism attacked religion, particularly Christianity, because it believed Christianity was filled with superstitions, but at least modernism believed that truth and it was not afraid to say so.[18]

On the surface, the one remaining thing between pre-modernism and modernism that linked them was the pursuit of objective truth:

> In the United States and the West, the previous era was defined by the constant pursuit of truth. That era was an uneven but upward climb toward truth. It lasted more than one thousand years, from the founding of Oxford University and the other early Christian universities until very recently. Within that era, the pursuit of truth was the light that guided Western scientists, innovators, educators, inventors, and lawmakers to constantly improve the human condition in Europe, the United States, and then the rest of the world. These people were imperfect, but their

---

18. Erwin W. Lutzer, *Who Are You to Judge?: Learning to Distinguish between Truths, Half-truths, and Lies*, kindle ed. (Chicago: Moody Press, 2002), 18.

pursuit of a higher truth beyond themselves produced contributions far beyond their own capacities.[19]

Nevertheless, this relentless pursuit of truth departed into two worlds between which there is a vast unpassable divide. The one group believed and taught for millennia that God revealed to us what we did not know and could not know about the world, humanity, and the problem and that the solution was found in God. The written Word of God is His written testament revealing the facts of this reality. The later modernist group said yes, there is truth, but only knowable through empiricism and man's reasoning. There is no God or divine revelation. The pre-modern and modern eras were then toppled in secular society by yet another belief system that continues to leave significant damage in its wake today.

Postmodernism

After the turn of the century and at the peak of the utopian-hopeful humanist and modernist progression, major world disasters began to unfold before the world. The cataclysmic events, such as the sinking of the unsinkable Titanic, the Stock Market crash and subsequent Great Depression, two World Wars, the Holocaust, the rise of communism and socialism, and nuclear weapons, all bent then broke the ideals and hopes of modernism.

The modernist's idea of man's endless ambition, self-assurance, and boundless optimism based on his power and intellect began to

19. Dickerson, *Hope of Nations*, 14.

erode. "The hopes that modernity had underscored, the triumph of 'Reason' and 'Science' that many thought would bring in utopia, have failed in almost every respect."[20] This failure then gave way to the formation of a new set of ideals concerning truth and reality and became known as *postmodernism.*

Postmodernism also caught more wind in its sails in colleges and universities through the United States and Europe in the 1970s, 80's and '90s, specifically in the areas of literary criticism. There were many thinkers in this area of study in the twentieth century, but one example stands out as Jacques Derrida explains:

> One was Derrida's theory of "deconstructing" literature, whereby we cannot rely on the idea that an author knew what he or she "meant" in a text so we must break it apart and examine it as a function of the political, social, historical, and cultural assumptions behind it . . . This idea was soon embraced by sociologists and others who got caught up in the idea that it should apply not just to literary texts but far more broadly, since, in a sense, everything could be interpreted as a "text." War, religion, economic relations, sexuality—indeed virtually all of human behavior was freighted with meanings that may or may not be understood by the actors who were engaging in them.[21]

Precise descriptions of postmodernism are varied, and at times, hard to define (which only proves the postmodernist's point).

20. D.A. Carson, ed., *Telling the Truth: Evangelizing Postmoderns*, kindle ed. (Grand Rapids, Mich: Zondervan, 2000), 10.

21. Lee McIntyre, *Post-Truth*, kindle ed., The MIT Press Essential Knowledge Series (Cambridge, MA: MIT Press, 2018), Location 1939.

Nevertheless, the following is an accurate description of postmodernism and its relation to truth by pastor and author Dennis McCallum:

> Postmodernists believe that truth is created, not discovered. They think things like reason, rationality, and confidence in science are cultural biases. They contend that those who trust reason-and things based on reason, like science, Western education, and governmental structures-unknowingly act out their European cultural conditioning. This conditioning seeks to keep power in the hands of the social elite.[22]

In the postmodern mentality, this is something to be regarded with suspicion leading to rejection altogether because "...all knowledge claims are really just an assertion of authority; they are a bullying tactic used by the powerful to force those who are weaker to accept their ideological views."[23]

Postmodernism saw a failure in man's self- advancement and convictions. Postmodernists could no longer accept what someone said or wrote in a definitive or absolute manner. They distrusted not only the authority of such individuals who assert absolutes but doubt even the process of coming to those kinds of conclusions. "The postmodernist approach is one in which everything is questioned, and little is taken at face value. There is no right answer, only narrative."[24]

22. Dennis McCallum, ed., *The Death of Truth* (Minneapolis, Minn: Bethany House Publishers, 1996), Location 140.
23.. McIntyre, *Post-Truth*, Location 1958.
24. McIntyre, *Post-Truth*, Location 1949.

Dr. D.A. Carson gives a descriptive explanation of postmodernism compared to modernism:

> Modernism is often pictured as pursuing truth, absolutism, linear thinking, rationalism, certainty, the cerebral as opposed to the affective—which in turn breeds arrogance, inflexibility, a lust to be right, the desire to control. Postmodernism, by contrast, recognizes how much of what we "know" is shaped (or constructed) by the culture in which we live, is controlled by emotions, aesthetics and heritage, and in fact can only be intelligently held as part of a common tradition, without overbearing claims to being true or right.[25]

Postmodernism did not just create an epistemological agnosticism toward how absolute truth claims are formed. It also brought about an innate, overwhelming doubt as to the truthfulness of objective truth claims and reality altogether:

> Post-modern philosophers preferred to understand language and culture as 'social constructs,' political phenomena that reflected the distribution of power across class, race, gender, and sexuality, rather than the abstract ideals of classical philosophy. And if everything is a 'social construct,' then who is to say what is false?[26]

Additionally, all we are doing is interpreting reality through our own subjective filters, assuring that claims to truth by one person rise

---

25. Carson, *Becoming Conversant With*, Location 317.
26. d'Ancona, *Post Truth*, 91.

to no higher level than that of another. There is no real rule by which to declare specific ideas as either right or wrong.

Postmodernism does not have (nor have use for) an objective, transcendent standard for all to conform to because the moral authority of that standard is questionable by default. Without an objective higher standard of truth, competing truths in the same context cannot genuinely be ruled wrong or right, or as superior one to another.

Additionally, postmodernism's distrust of absolute truth claims lends itself to two contradictory ideas claiming to be true at the same time. This is a clear violation of the most basic and undeniable *Law of Non-contradiction*. "The law of non-contradiction states that contradictory claims cannot both be true at the same time in the same sense. If we conclude that something is false, then we know its opposite is true. Simply put, the opposite of true is false."[27] The axiom of postmodernism is already self-defeating from the outset.

To the idea of there being absolute truth, the postmodernist dismisses it with a simple wave of the magic wand, denying reality, and thus creating and defending a defenseless artificial standard. In other words, a postmodernist insists there is no truth, then ask if that is true for everyone else, including the postmodernist! It is a self-defeating argument for the postmodernist to make a truth claim when he says there are no truth claims.

---

27. Steven Garofolo, *Right for You, but Not for Me: A Response to Moral Relativism*, kindle ed. (Charlotte, NC: TriedStone Publishing Company, 2013), 204.

At least within modernism, there was a binding hierarchy of knowledge that the populace generally recognized from their national leadership and thinking:

> Moreover, if we would still like to try to define the truth in those periods, we should probably use the already mentioned construction of the hierarchy of knowledge... where the hierarchy was characterized by those that could implement amongst the masses their version of the truth...[28]

In postmodernism, there are no generally accepted or authoritatively endorsed hierarchies, nor do they believe should there be.

The postmodernist has focused on his established mission of what they call *deconstruction.* They believe that all truth hierarchies are just constructed by local societal groups based solely on their local subsets of subjective ideals. Therefore, these constructed ideas are valueless and unenforceable on others. The postmodernist's mission, therefore, was (and remains) to deconstruct, or tear down these socially constructed ideals. Over the last several decades, with methodical subtlety, they have permeated the strategically influential institutions to turn the world postmodern.

> ... since its emergence during the latter half of the twentieth century, postmodernism has infiltrated many key areas of thought including philosophy, the arts, literature, history,

28. Diego Han, "From Postmodernity to a Post-Truth Society," *Journal of Comparative Studies* (2018), 4.

sociology, psychology, inter-cultural studies, and increasingly, technology. Its influence, especially in academia, is strong and continues to grow. Therefore, it demands our attention.[29]

They have been incredibly successful and have steered the West to think, speak, act, and even create in postmodern fashion. However, there is a paradox in their mission: In the postmodernist's effort to deconstruct all presumed traditional hierarchies to which compliance was demanded, the postmodernist creates new hierarchies to which they demand compliance!

Additionally, when it comes to the area of morality and ethics, postmodern thinking puts forward the idea that "morality is not a matter of objectivity but narrow, personal bias."[30] The natural outcome of this thinking disregards the presence of a transcendent, perfect, and objective moral Law-Giver who gives us the Laws and standards to judge right and wrong. The natural result is that each person's individually concocted ideas of what is right and wrong now take over as truth. If sufficient numbers of individuals with authority and influence generally agree on the same ideas of what is right and wrong, they can effectively sway the majority of the populace to accept (or conform) to the same.

The first stumbling block for this subjectivism is that the beliefs they hold for the moment may (and usually will) change in the next generations to come. Thus, what is rejected today can likely be considered acceptable just a few years down the road. This portends

29. Phillips, Brown, and Stonestreet, *Making Sense Of*, 49.
30. Lutzer, *Who Are You*, 169.

a domino effect of constant erosion in that culture's values and integrity, fomenting itself in a limitlessly tragic manner.

The changing of beliefs and feelings in differing contexts, disregarding an objective truth standard to keep them grounded, is what is called *relativism*. "Briefly stated, moral relativism is the view that moral judgments, beliefs about right and wrong, good and bad, not only vary greatly across time and contexts, but that their correctness is dependent on or relative to individual or cultural perspectives and frameworks."[31]

The famous atheist of the nineteenth century Friedrich Nietzsche put it this way: "You have your way. I have my way. As for the right way, the correct way, the only way: it does not exist."[32] Possessing the twins of relativism and subjectivism, postmodernism has long been large and in charge. It has permeated academia, the media, social media, ethics, language, politics, legislation, science, and even religion.

Whereas postmodernism remains a force with a clear denunciation of both premodernism and modernism, the current post-truth era can be described as either being born from postmodernism or as the proverbial phoenix rising from the ashes of a disjointed, impoverished and failed postmodern rationale. Post-truth intends to finish what postmodernism could not.

31. Maria Baghramian, "Relativism," Stanford Encyclopedia of Philosophy, Winter 2018, accessed March 11, 2019,

   http://plato.stanford.edu/archives/win2018/entries/relativism.

32. Beverly A. Potter and Mark J. Estren, *Question Authority to Think for Yourself,* kindle ed. (Oakland, CA: Ronin Publishing,, 2012), 492.

Depending on which cultural observer one hears, postmodernism still is considered the source of either tremendous positive change or the slippery slide downward in Western culture today. Many contain the recognition of its progeny, known as post-truth, primarily within the political sphere and not a distinct and central force distinguished from postmodernism. Abdu Murray, in his groundbreaking book *Saving Truth*, makes a clear and concise explanation of the distinction between postmodernism and post-truth:

> Where postmodernism failed because it was inherently incoherent, the post-truth mindset may succeed because it is not. It faces the problem of truth head-on. Unlike postmodernism, the post-truth mindset acknowledges objective truth, but subordinates it to preferences. That's dangerous, as logic and evidence don't have the same influence over the post-truth mindset that they had over a postmodern.[33]

Post-truth is a distinct worldview that now pretends to be the foundational mindset for the world to fill the vacuum that previous religions and philosophies have been unsuccessful in filling satisfactorily. Post-truth is now *the* overall dominant force that is presently driving societal thinking and expression. Now we will see, in the following chapters, the steering wheel of Western culture, which post-truth has taken hold of and mercilessly steers in the direction it pleases.

33. Abdu Murray, *Saving Truth: Finding Meaning & Clarity in a Post-truth World*, kindle ed. (Grand Rapids, Michigan: Zondervan, 2018), 14.

Chapter 5

Post-truth in Politics

Perhaps nowhere else is the prominence of post-truth seen and heard the most than in the area of politics. Post-truth politics as a term, itself, has also been called post-reality politics[1] and post-factual politics.[2] The credit for the astronomical rise in the term post-truth

1. Jack Holmes, "George Will: "Post-Factual Politics" From Campaign Still Exists, Nixon More Of A Statesman Than Current Leadership," Esquire, September 26, 2016, accessed September 21, 2019,
   https://www.realclearpolitics.com/video/2016/11/28/george_will_post-
   https://www.esquire.com/news-politics/news/a48906/trump-campaign-
   manager-lester-holt/.

2. Ian Schwartz, "George Will: "Post-Factual Politics" From Campaign Still Exists, Nixon More Of A Statesman Than Current Leadership," Politics, Real Clear

itself is usually due to its political usage, especially during the 2016 presidential election in the United States, along with the concurrent Brexit campaign in the United Kingdom.

Lies, deception, and half-truths in politics have existed for thousands of years, yet this post-truth era stands out in Western culture in the historical timeline. There are still lingering accusations from both sides of the aisle, claiming that lies were told blatantly and viciously to win the mind of the voter.

Joshua Forstenzer of the University of Sheffield (UK) gives a straightforward definition for post-truth politics: "...the post-truth character of our politics refers to the relative irrelevance of the value of truth in contemporary public affairs."[3] Appeals to emotion, fueled by podium rhetoric and effective media advertisement, created a daily whirlwind of convincing the masses of something before fact-checking can catch up to it or prevent it. As the old saying goes, "A lie gets halfway around the world before the truth has a chance to get its pants on." Populism thrives on this type of thing, whether the motivations are pure or not. The notion that the end justifies the means would be the mantra of any person or organization perpetuating post-truth idealism.

Politics, November 28, 2016, accessed September 21, 2019, http://www.realclearpolitics.com/video/2016/11/28/george_will_post-factual_politics_from_campaign_nixon_statesman_trump.html.

3. Joshua Forstenzer, *Something Has Cracked: Post-Truth*, ed. Tony Saich, Ash Center Occasional Papers Series (University of Sheffield (UK): Ash Center for Democratic Governance and Innovation-Harvard Kenedy School, 2018).

During and since the presidential election of 2016, voices in the media, the internet, and literature, place almost exclusive blame on President Trump for promoting post-truth lies. The question remains, is this a legitimate clarion call from the grassroots of the nation for real truth to be seen and heard in our political leaders? Or, is it merely the vehement reaction of left-leaning mainstream institutions, aghast at being seriously challenged for the first time, after decades of being the self-appointed truth-bearers?

One prominent example of post-truth in politics was viewed after President Trump had repeated the claim that his inauguration had the highest attendance of any other in history. Afterward, in a White House press conference, then-press secretary, Sean Spicer, defended the president's claim. Following that, White House counselor to the president Kellyanne Conway was asked in a TV interview about the claim, and she said that Spicer had given "alternative facts."[4] Both sides, left and right, vociferously defended or attacked the justification for such a description of the claim.

Unfortunately, the real facts were muffled in all the hubris leaving *alternative facts* as a jocular word to point out only one truthful set of facts exists. The conundrum as to which truth is the real truth is now an everyday battle, one which will be discussed further in this book.

4. Alexandra Jaffe, "Kellyanne Conway: WH Spokesman Gave 'Alternative Facts' on Inauguration Crowd," News, NBCnews.com, January 22, 2017, accessed August 3, 2019, https://www.nbcnews.com/storyline/meet-the-press-70-years/wh-spokesman-gave-alternative-facts-inauguration-crowd-n710466.

We have seen lies exposed in modern American politics with such historical examples as presidents Richard Nixon (Watergate), Ronald Reagan (Iran-Contra affair), George H. W. Bush ("read my lips, no new taxes") Bill Clinton (Monica Lewinsky affair), George W. Bush (weapons of mass destruction never found in Iraq), Barak Obama ("you can keep your insurance"), not to mention a myriad of many lesser political figures with at least one major lie attached to them for their entire lives. We are not shocked by this, nor is it an attribute of just post-truth. Therein lies the problem, which is an unfortunate characteristic of post-truth: that we often acquiesce to what's being said and done because we sense we cannot change it. Sometimes we even collude with it:

> Yet political lies, spin and falsehood are emphatically not the same as Post-Truth. What is new is not the mendacity of politicians but the public's response to it. Outrage gives way to indifference and, finally, to collusion. Lying is regarded as the norm even in democracies... We no longer expect our elected politicians to speak the truth: that, for now, has been written out of the job description, or at least significantly relegated on the list of required attributes.[5]

David Roberts, founder and editor of the left-leaning Grist.org, made this statement after reviewing political science studies on the choice of candidates to vote for: "We live in post-truth politics: a political culture in which politics (public opinion and media narratives) have become almost entirely disconnected from policy

5. d'Ancona, *Post Truth*, 28.

(the substance of legislation). This dims any hope of reasoned legislative compromise."[6] It is significant that many on both the left and right sides of the philosophical and political spectrum are starting to agree on this observation.

Most potential voters do little to no basic research to find the real facts. They have little interest in serious research or applying actual critical thinking to make reasonable conclusions. Instead, the average voter settles for the slick epithets by campaign strategists who seek to trigger our emotions to solidify a reaction and vote. "In the West, it is emotional connection – always part of political decision-making – that threatens to eclipse our inherited insistence upon the truth as the main criterion in political contests."[7]

Major political governing decisions are often being made based not on accurate facts and research but rather on emotions and pithy sound bites pumped into minds by those who vie for power. To quote d' Ancona again: "…emotion is reclaiming its primacy and truth is in retreat."[8] That fittingly describes post-truth politics.

6. David Roberts, "Post-truth Politics," Grist.org, April 1, 2010, accessed August 8, 2019, https://grist.org/article/2010-03-30-post-truth-politics/.

7. d'Ancona, *Post Truth*, 27.

8. d'Ancona, *Post Truth*, 31.

Chapter 6

Post-Truth in the Media

> "Amendment I - Congress shall make no law respecting an
> establishment of religion or prohibiting the free exercise thereof;
> or abridging the freedom of speech, or of the press; or the right
> of the people peaceably to assemble, and to petition the
> government for a redress of grievances. The bastion of any
> democracy or republic is the freedom of free speech. The ability
> to freely speak up and out is necessary and is enshrined in our
> very Constitution."[1]

The guaranteed right of a free press and free speech is essential to the
foundation of any democracy or republic. Today that principle is

1. *US Constitution.* Amendment 1.

mostly enjoyed by the press and the media, specifically the news outlets, be it in print or digital form.

The golden age of the press, from the early 1960s till the early 1980s, is the time when the three major TV networks and the major newspapers and magazines across the U.S. held the monopoly on information gathering and broadcasting. Then in 1980, cable TV opened up the whole new world of the 24-hour news network, starting with CNN. Throughout this period, people had no choice but to listen to and accept as true whatever the single viewpoint of major media had to say about what was happening in the nation and the world every day.

Then from the 1990s and continuing till today, the explosive advent of conservative AM talk radio, the internet, and social media opened up an almost limitless world of grass-roots voices, news sources, commentators, podcasts, and videos, worldwide. All this was cheaply and instantly accessible through computers, smartphones, and TV. In a short amount of time, that one voice was drowned out by the innumerable others, regardless of the quality or veracity of what they were saying. With the exponentially growing amount of watching eyes and eager critics through social media, the press itself has become regularly accustomed to crafting the truth to fit the desired narrative.

Along with the press, Hollywood and media celebrities shoulder a large portion of the responsibility for the state of post-truth we are in today. The TV and movie industry has been the ideologues' playground for broadcasting selective values and beliefs through entertainment. "As a see-no-evil, hear-no-evil medium, television is not just susceptible to deception but downright collusive."[2] Peter Keyes tells how Hollywood and the entertainment industry unduly influence the non-fictional genre of television. He shows how they do this by watering down the facts of a real-life story, using what works, and making it more dramatic than real life. One example he gives of this is ABC's Roone Arledge (1931-2002) and how he made such contortions successful in the entertainment media:

> Arledge was the architect of melodramatized sports broadcasts and news shows. His genius lay in integrating fictional storytelling techniques with material that was supposedly factual. In time all of television followed Arledge's lead. Even public television succumbed to the temptation to improve on facts, as they did in Liberators, a PBS documentary about two all-black army units that supposedly helped liberate the Dachau and Buchenwald concentration camps. "We were nowhere near these camps when they were liberated," said a veteran of the 761st Tank Battalion, one of two units featured in this film. "I first went to Buchenwald in 1991 with PBS, not the 761st." A former army captain who commanded C Company, the other unit featured, said he and his men were sixty miles away from Dachau on the day they allegedly took part in its liberation. (The documentary was withdrawn.)"[3]

In the 2002 movie *Spiderman,* the iconic phrase spoken by the fictitious Uncle Ben is well remembered: "With great power comes

2. Keyes, *The Post-Truth Era*, Location 2428.
3. Keyes, *The Post-Truth Era*, Location 2422.

great responsibility." Ironically, the very medium that produced such a truthful script line is, itself, unabashedly guilty of creating a world where facts and truth may exist, but they do not matter. What matters to the celebrity media is how individuals make their set of facts believed and felt through dramatic story regardless of its accuracy to the original true story.

A newly coined term emerged during the presidential election of 2016. The term *fake news* began to be used popularly as then-presidential Republican candidate Trump pointed out certain falsehoods being reported about himself and his campaign. Others accused his campaign of doing the same.

In another instance, then president-elect Donald Trump made pervasive use of the term after Hillary Clinton used it to point out false reports and their risks to people. "President-elect Trump took up the phrase the following month, in January 2017, a little over a week before taking office. In response to a question, he said: "you're fake news" to CNN reporter Jim Acosta. Around the same time he started repeating the phrase on Twitter."[4]

How is "fake news" defined? "'Fake news' is not simply news that is false; it is deliberately false."[5] It is misinformation that is created with no facts, or at best, half-truths inserted in the mix to fit a specific narrative or storyline. It comes in the form of social media posts, news articles stories, and even entire websites that have been

4. Mike Wendling, "The (almost) complete history of 'fake news,'" BBC Trending, January 22, 2018, accessed August 3, 2019, https://www.bbc.com/news/blogs-trending-42724320.

5. McIntyre, *Post-Truth*, Location 1549.

faked in order to propagate such material. David Lazer, Political Science and Computer and Information Science at Northeastern University, wrote:

> Fake news has been around for many years since the beginning of the Gutenberg. We define "fake news" to be fabricated information that mimics news media content in form but not in organizational process or intent. Fake-news outlets, in turn, lack the news media's editorial norms and processes for ensuring the accuracy and credibility of information. Fake news overlaps with other information disorders, such as misinformation (false or misleading information) and disinformation (false information that is purposely spread to deceive people).[6]

Fake news usually is not created by well-meaning people who made an honest error in their facts, which can easily be retracted, corrected, and forgiven and forgotten. Fake news, as the definition states, is deliberate. The intended purpose of the creators of such false information was not even to spread an ideology – its purpose was originally to make money. They put up an onscreen ad sure to trigger emotional reactions according to whom they targeted the ads, whether to the left or right of the political spectrum. Their purpose? To make money off of Google and Facebook ads!

The original motive was an intentional act of a mislead-for-profit scheme, carried out by an unscrupulous cottage-industry of

6. David M. J. Lazer et al., "The Science of Fake News," *Science* 359, no. 6380 (March 2018), accessed August 13, 2019,
http://science.sciencemag.org/content/359/6380/1094.

online entrepreneurship. It quickly caught on as a deliberate political tactic done just for ideological purposes and as a tool of misinformation from outside (and subsequently inside) the U.S.:

> At the beginning of the 2016 election season, perhaps that purpose was "clickbait." They wanted you to click on a provocative headline so that you would add a few cents to their coffers, in much the same way that the National Enquirer entices you to slip it into your grocery cart with headlines such as "Hillary: Six Months to Live!" But then the darkness descended. Some of the creators of "fake news" began to notice that the favorable stories about Trump were getting many more clicks than the favorable ones about Hillary—and that the negative stories about Hillary were getting the most clicks of all. So guess which ones they doubled down on? In this environment, fake news evolved from clickbait to disinformation. It morphed from a vehicle for financial gain to one for political manipulation. A good deal of fake news in the 2016 election originated from the Balkans and other parts of Eastern Europe.[7]

There have been numerous revelations of fake news being committed by several major (and many lesser) news media outlets. They create a preconceived and targeted storyline – or narrative – they want to achieve and then fill it in with stories that are molded to fit their ideal. Real *narrative journalism* (also called *literary journalism*[8])

7. McIntyre, *Post-Truth*, Location 1555.

8. Rachel Deahl, "What Is Narrative Journalism?," Glossary, the balancecareers, December 20, 2018, accessed August 20, 2019, https://www.thebalancecareers.com/what-is-narrative-journalism-2316035.

has been responsibly accomplished, serving as an interesting way to tell a true story. It has served as a journalistic way of describing people, places, and a long series of events in an immersive way that reads like fiction. It is not originally intended as a tool conforming others to a particular personal or group agenda. "Ultimately, the primary goal of the creative nonfiction writer is to communicate information, just like a reporter, but to shape it in a way that reads like fiction."[9]

Unfortunately, in recent years, the challenges to narrative, or literary, journalism to remain truthful, factual, and without a damaging agenda, have eroded rapidly due to ideological and political pressures, among other reasons. As this has occurred, a natural outgrowth is called *confirmation bias.* "Confirmation bias, as the term is typically used in the psychological literature, connotes the seeking or interpreting of evidence in ways that are partial to existing beliefs, expectations, or a hypothesis in hand."[10] In other words, confirmation bias is when the individual looks for and proposes evidence that will only support his or her predetermined beliefs or preconceptions. This is a form of virulent post-truth. Dan Shellee, executive director of the Radio Television Digital News Association comments on this:

9. Margot Singer and Nicole Walker, eds., *Bending Genre: Essays on Creative Nonfiction* (New York: Bloomsbury, 2013), 3.

10. Raymond S. Nickerson, "Confirmation Bias: A Ubiquitous Phenomenon in Many Guises," *Review of General Psychology* 2, no. 2 (1998): 175, accessed September 3, 2019,
http://psy2.ucsd.edu/~mckenzie/nickersonConfirmationBias.pdf.

Too many people think what they see on some cable networks' early-morning and/or prime-time lineups, what they hear on talk radio, and what they read on newspapers' editorial pages are the facts. Period. Such content certainly contains facts, but those facts are almost always used to reinforce the purveyor's predetermined point of view, or detract from points of view that conflict with their own.[11]

The increase in several news media outlets to walk back, or retract, statements, or even entire stories, has brought on a great distrust of the media by the American public. In one recent clear example of post-truth narrative journalism, a reporter in an MSNBC interview on-air reported that President Trump had loan documents which had Russian oligarchs as co-signers. The problem, revealed within less than one day, was that this information came only from one source and was unverified through normal fact-checking procedures. The reporter ended up having to make a full on-air retraction and apology the following day.[12]

This kind of reporting, where misinformation or unverified information is published rapidly to the public to hit a targeted

11. Dan Shelley, "A huge problem for trust in journalism: Opinion media," Radio Television Digital News Association-RTNA, November 2, 2017, accessed August 20, 2019, http://rtdna.org/article/a_huge_problem_for_trust_in_journalism_opinion_medi a.

12. John Koblin, "Lawrence O'Donnell Retracts Claim of Russians' Role in Trump Loans," *he New York Times*, August 28, 2019, accessed September 3, 2019, https://www.nytimes.com/2019/08/28/business/media/lawrence-odonnell-trump-claims.html.

negative agenda, has happened on both left- and right-wing news sites. It constitutes another post-truth maneuver that intentionally appeals to emotion and preference for specified beliefs without regard to the actual truth and facts.

In a joint Gallup and Knight Foundation Survey done of 1,400 Gallup Poll members, it was discovered that "Overall, Americans believe 62% of the news they see on television, read in newspapers and hear on the radio is biased…Americans tend to think the majority of news reporting is accurate, but they still believe a substantial percentage of it, 44%, is inaccurate."[13] Many fake news stories abound of which these are just a few examples:

> One of the more bizarre fake news stories was "Pizzagate," a convoluted and slanderous online conspiracy theory connecting Hillary Clinton and her aides to a nonexistent child-trafficking ring run out of a real pizza restaurant. It convinced at least one person who showed up at the restaurant to investigate armed with a rifle…a Knoxville newspaper reported that a terminally ill child had died in the arms of an actor playing Santa Claus. The paper has since retracted the story, but not before it "went viral."[14]

13. John Kinsellagh, "Perceived accuracy and bias in the news media," Knight Foundation, June 20, 2018, accessed August 20, 2019, http://knightfoundation.org/reports/perceived-accuracy-and-bias-in-the-news-media.

14. Phil Mobley, "Post-truth (And Consequences)," In The World, Online Magazine of the Presbyterian Church of America-byFaith, November 27, 2018,

In another instance of many:

> Back in 2004, The Boston Globe published, on its front page, sexually graphic images that purported to show U.S. soldiers raping Iraqi women. The images were abhorrent and unleashed a torrent of criticism of American soldiers in Iraq.
>
> The only problem was the photograph was a fake. Then-editor Marty Baron said, "There was a lapse in judgment and procedures." The much touted editorial firewalls and protections for reporting integrity were completely ineffectual. The reason the photograph made it through the editorial safeguards was that those charged with ensuring reporting integrity accepted the photograph as true, because they *wanted* it to be true. Authentication was unnecessary because the image comported with their view that U.S. soldiers were engaged in acts of barbarism and torture.[15]

It needs to be interjected here that there are openly declared satirical websites that produce ironic and humorous news-like stories to poke fun at or humorously expose ridiculous events or faulty actions by celebrities or organizations. These websites are not fake news or misinformation and are not included in the post-truth discussion. Surprisingly, their writing seems so realistic many times

accessed August 20, 2019,

https://dictionary.cambridge.org/us/dictionary/english/post-truth.

15. John Kinsellagh, "Fake News and the Narrative," American Thinker, January 25, 2019, accessed August 20, 2019,

http://www.americanthinker.com/articles/2019/01/fake_news_and_the_narrativ e.html.

that people have mistakenly perceived them as real news sources and posted them on social media.

The ubiquitous fake news phenomena not only comes from the left but at times from the right of the political spectrum. What is worse, there are professing Christians who also spread fake news. They are triggered by an ad or news story and they indiscriminately spread it online like anyone else. They have done this spuriously, without fact-checking it first, or weighing the actual moral gain or loss in posting it to others publicly. Whether on the left or right on the political scale, what incited them emotionally about the other resulted in an immediate and unverified sharing, or posting, of intentional misinformation peddled by dubious sources. This is quintessential post-truth, where emotions and preferred beliefs dominate actual empirical facts and reality.

Even if the story appears to be accurate and corroborated, Christians ought to be the most careful and cautious in their motive for passing such information to potentially thousands of others. If it does not serve any Gospel-related purpose then repeating the possible dubious information should be negated. As anything else communicated openly, once in public, those words cannot be withdrawn.

Christian apologist Abdu Murray relates an instance of conservative sloppiness in repeating false information as well as liberal sources have done. In 2016, Seth Rich, a young Democratic National Committee worker, was murdered. Even a year later, fake news of conspiracy theories about Rich's murder abounded, with many in the online Christian community doing much of the fake news peddling. "The barrage of conspiracy theories that followed his murder forced Seth Rich's parents to relive the tragedy."[16] In calling out the Christians propagating such untruths, Christian social commentator Ed Stetzer wrote an open rebuke:

> In Exodus 20:16, we are commanded, 'Do not give false testimony against your neighbor.' John Wesley described bearing false witness as 'speaking falsely in any matter,' including that which 'speak[s] unjustly against our neighbor, to the prejudice of his reputation.' And that's what you are doing if you are spreading these untruths."[17]

In another example of fake news from conservative Christian circles was the news of litigation that supposedly was aimed at outlawing the Bible as hate speech. Abdu Murray brings yet another instance to our attention:

> In mid-2015, my news and social media feeds were abuzz with urgent-seeming headlines bemoaning, "It's Already Starting!" and "That Didn't Take Long!" The articles insinuated that an LGBT activist leveraged the United States Supreme Court's decision in Obergefell v. Hodges legalizing same-sex marriage to file a federal lawsuit to outlaw the Bible as hate speech. Just three

16. Murray, *Saving Truth*, 40.

17. Ed Stetzer, "Christians, Repent (Yes, Repent) of Spreading Conspiracy Theories and Fake News—It's Bearing False Witness," Christianity Today-Exchange with Ed Stetzer, May 31, 2017, accessed August 4, 2019, http://www.christianitytoday.com/edstetzer/2017/may/christians-repent-conspiracy-theory-fake-news.html.

minutes of investigation revealed this narrative was bogus—and obviously so. Yes, a gay man filed a lawsuit in a Michigan federal court against two Christian publishers. But he did not seek to have the Bible "banned." He sought money for emotional distress, claiming the publishers had mistranslated the Bible to be unfavorable to homosexuals. And he didn't file his lawsuit after the Obergefell decision. He filed it in 2008—seven years before the Supreme Court's ruling. Not only that, but the lawsuit was dismissed almost as soon as it was filed. The judge, a principled jurist I had the privilege of appearing before as an attorney, dismissed the case because it had no basis in the law and was "largely incomprehensible." In less time than a TV commercial break, I learned that this alarmist story was false.[18]

When Christian and conservative individuals and organizations post information that is cobbled together to meet a preconceived agenda, it does not make them more credible or trustworthy just because they come from that end of the religious or political spectrum. On the contrary, it cheapens and devalues the very Judeo-Christian values they profess to stand upon. It validates the accusations of hypocrisy that the unbelieving opposition casts upon Christians and conservatives. More importantly, it besmirches the reputation and witness of the Creator of those values and His objective truth and holy character upon which it is based.

Suffice it to say, the institutional media news outlets, the Hollywood celebrity media industry, left-wing or right-wing bloggers, and secular or Christian commentators who spread such

18. Murray, *Saving Truth*, 28.

misinformation have had a shameful part in shaping and furthering our current post-truth culture.

Chapter 7

Post-truth in Academia

Academia, or the *academy*, is the term for the entire educational system with particular focus on the post-secondary level. Academia is not immune to post-truth influences. On the contrary, it is arguably the hotbed of the creation and leadership of post-truth ideals on the culture, politics, and all forms of the media. At the heart of the educational system's post-truth model is the idea that even when objective truth is revealed, it is dismissed in preference for one's own beliefs as the truth. It is yet again another manifestation of the *hard meaning* of post-truth as wherein actual objective truth is disregarded and a deliberate push to impose a false truth standard.

At academia's core, from which teaching and learning for now and the future is arduously tested and established by proven scholars, there has been a years-long *coup de 'tat* of leadership among the humanities and philosophy at university and scholarly levels. Their slow takeover of academic scholarship began with the postmodernists, most of whom are radicals from the declining social movements of the 1960s and 1970s. They continued their determined revolution of influence and power through the educational realm with a more intellectual and nuanced framework.

The absurd pseudo-scholarship they have produced is now at the helm of Western educational institutions with massive corruptive influence, especially and mostly in the humanities and social sciences. Many conservatives have long warned of this for decades, but many self-described liberals (in contrast to the extreme left), professors and media influencers agree, as well. Whistle-blowers of the post-truth hijacking of educational institutions and scholarship on both left and right have begun to talk to one another and have formed a loosely knit resistance to it.

Perhaps the most recent and profound example of this post-truth upheaval in education was fully revealed in the now-infamous *Grievance Studies Affair* that occurred in 2018.[1] The project was carried out by a team of three thinkers and educators: Peter Boghossian, an assistant professor of philosophy at Portland State University, James Lindsay, a philosopher and with a doctorate in

1. Jillian Kay Melchior, "Fake News Comes to Academia," *Wall Street Journal*,
   October 5, 2018, accessed August 27, 2019, http://www.wsj.com/articles/fake-news-comes-to-academia-1538520950.

math, and Helen Pluckrose, of London, England, a scholar of English literature and history and editor of AreoMagazine.com.

They were alarmed by the erosion of true scholarship and education by the leaders of what they dubbed *grievance studies* and were determined to expose it.

By grievance studies they mean, "Scholarship based less upon finding truth and more upon attending to social grievances."[2] The grievance studies definition presented by the three will be further explored in particular later on in this book.

Their purpose was clear and was meant to send a message to the educational, scholarly elite at the university level:

> We undertook this project to study, understand, and expose the reality of grievance studies, which is corrupting academic research. Because open, good-faith conversation around topics of identity such as gender, race, and sexuality (and the scholarship that works with them) is nearly impossible, our aim has been to reboot these conversations. We hope this will give people— especially those who believe in liberalism, progress, modernity, open inquiry, and social justice —a clear reason to look at the identitarian madness coming out of the academic and activist left and say, 'No, I will not go along with that. You do not speak for me.'[3]

2. James A. Lindsay, Peter Boghossian, and Helen Pluckrose, "Academic Grievance Studies and the Corruption of Scholarship," Aero, October 2, 2018, accessed August 20, 2019, http://areomagazine.com/2018/10/02/academic-grievance-studies-and-the-corruption-of-scholarship/.

3. Lindsay, Boghossian, and Pluckrose, *Academic Grievance Studies.*

Their scheme began in October of 2017 and involved writing 20 essays or papers on different subjects within the current grievance studies framework. They submitted their work to the normal process in the upper-level educational proving grounds, but the papers they submitted were absolute hoaxes. They wrote the papers using pseudonyms. Many of the sources they referenced were fictional, as well as the actual research. Much of their writing also used shoddy methodologies and incorrectly used terminology. They chose absurd subjects and ideas (often using sexual themes and terminology) applying them to academic and real-world grievance studies issues.

One such example of their hoax papers that attained acceptance was entitled *Title: Our Struggle is My Struggle: Solidarity Feminism as an Intersectional Reply to Neoliberal and Choice Feminism.* The authors Maria Gonzalez, Ph.D., and Lisa A. Jones, Ph.D., of the Feminist Activist Collective for Truth (FACT) were both fictional. Their thesis was "Thesis: That feminism which foregrounds individual choice and responsibility and female agency and strength can be countered by a feminism which unifies in solidarity around the victimhood of the most marginalized women in society."[4] Their tactic in this original paper was to take a chapter from Hitler's *Mein Kampf* and replace specific Nazi terms with extreme feminist catchwords and then mix in well-constructed (albeit fake and irrational) arguments. They received reviews reflecting sincere accolades to its theorizing and other reviewers giving suggestions to tweak the paper as it went to being published.

4. Lindsay, Boghossian, and Pluckrose, *Academic Grievance Studies.*

What is most remarkable is that their groundbreaking effort was not written from the world view that one would expect. There is no input from a conservative (or even Christian) socio-political think tank, academic group, or media personality. No conservative or Christian academic was ever involved in this project at any moment. All three of the creators have unequivocally and openly established that they are liberals.[5] This was done from within the ranks of university thinking and writing as liberals, which gives its validity even greater significance and impact.

They took on this homemade enterprise at risk of their reputations and awaited to see that, once submitted to various journals and scholars, they would be peer-reviewed. The holy grail of their intentions was to see how many of their false papers would not only be peer-reviewed but published as well.

Their pioneering project was eventually sniffed out about halfway through their endeavor by Wall Street Journal editorial page writer Ms. Jillian Kay Melchior. Up and until the Wall Street Journal exposed it, they had seven of the twenty papers accepted for peer-review, complete with applause and constructive comments from the scholarly reviewers. In the end, four were published online with the other three awaiting publication. Scholarly submissions like these typically take three to six months or more to go from acceptance to review and then to publication.[6] They were stunned and exuberant to

5. Lindsay, Boghossian, and Pluckrose, *Academic Grievance Studies*.
6. Lindsay, Boghossian, and Pluckrose, *Academic Grievance Studies*.

receive the news of their acceptance and public publishing.[7] What have been the effects of this project? Does it have a real-world impact at all, or was it done in obscurity? Does it prove their claims about the corruption within the scholarship of postmodernism (and additionally, post-truth)?

First, the acceptance of their articles confirmed their fears and publicly proved the proverbial *emperor has no clothes* in the vast majority of scholarship and education within the humanities and within feminine, gender, queer, fat, postcolonial, anticolonial, social justice and other related theories and studies. Furthermore, the trio of educators confirmed what their core suspicion was from the beginning: from within the scholarship of these grievance studies' journals and their scholars, there exists a systemic disregard and failure to maintain the high standard needed for the production and protection of knowledge in our society as a whole. Dr. Lindsay elaborates:

> Based on our data, there is a problem occurring with knowledge production within fields that have been corrupted by grievance studies arising from critical constructivism and radical skepticism. Among the problems are how topics like race, gender, sexuality, society, and culture are researched. Perhaps most concerning is how the current highly ideological disciplines undermine the value of more rigorous work being done on these topics and erodes confidence in the university system. Research

7. Mike Naya, Academics expose corruption in Grievance Studies, YouTube Video, 00:05, Filmed October 2, 2018, accessed September 21, 2019, http://www.youtube.com/watch?v=kVk9a5Jcd1k&t=76s.

into these areas is crucial, and it must be rigorously conducted and minimize ideological influences. The further results on these topics diverge from reality, the greater chance they will hurt those their scholarship is intended to help.

Worse, the problem of corrupt scholarship has already leaked heavily into other fields like education, social work, media, psychology, and sociology-among others—and it openly aims to continue spreading. This makes the problem a grave concern that's rapidly undermining the legitimacy and reputations of universities, skewing politics, drowning out needed conversations, and pushing the culture war to ever more toxic and existential polarization. Further, it is affecting activism on behalf of women and racial and sexual minorities in a way which is counterproductive to equality aims by feeding into right-wing reactionary opposition to those equality objectives.[8]

Apart from the trio's comments on right-wing and left-wing issues, their concerns are the same as those of us in conservative evangelicalism when it comes to post-truth activism. Post-truth activism includes many of the connected post-truth ideologies and themes such as intersectionality, racism (according to its post-truth definition), white privilege, toxic masculinity, equity, gender, feminine issues, and others, which will be analyzed in the next chapter.

For their involvement in this exposé, these liberal professors have experienced a substantial backlash from many in the academy, social media, and the blogosphere. For Lindsay and Pluckrose, they

8. Lindsay, Boghossian, and Pluckrose, *Academic Grievance Studies.*

continue to endure heavy criticism, although due to being independent of any academic governance they have not been disciplined in any way.

Peter Boghossian (a faculty member at Portland State University at the time of their writing project) has endured the harshest repercussions. After the heavy criticism by an anonymous group of faculty members Boghossian received from the campus newspaper, proceedings began in January by Portland State University administration against him.[9] In the end, he was deemed in violation of rules on human-subjects research with his punishment, including a ban from involvement in any campus research projects, required attendance in the "protection of human subjects training," and placed on administrative leave (with severance pay) until mid-December 2019.[10] The three educators continue joint and separate public appearances in the various media outlets promoting their ongoing struggle against the malaise at the university-level and in the culture at large.

The effect of the aforesaid post-truth ideologies in university-level academia trickles down to the teachers of local schools at all levels, even to kindergarten. Many professors indoctrinate, instead of

9. Letter to the Editor, "Conceptual Penises' and other trolling," PSU Vanguard, November 9, 2018, accessed October 21, 2019, http://psuvanguard.com/conceptual-penises-and-other-trolling/.

10. Peter Wood and David Randall, "Portland State U Punishes Professor For Proving Gender Studies Is A Joke," Federalist, last modified August 30, 2019, accessed October 21, 2019, https://thefederalist.com/2019/08/30/portland-state-u-punishes-professor-proving-gender-studies-joke/.

educate, the minds and emotions of the students without regard to genuine critical thinking.

One of the main adverse effects of this brainwashing is the avoidance, and suppression, of allowing speeches and forums by conservative, and even some liberal, speakers invited by student-led organizations of different persuasions on university campuses. Some of those affected have been notable speakers such as former Senator and Attorney General Jeff Sessions[11], British, gay, far-right political commentator and speaker Miles Yanapolous,[12] conservative Jewish political commentator and author Ben Shapiro,[13] and Jewish, gay, political commentator and talk show host Dave Rubin,[14] among many others. This type of censorship (also called *no-platforming*) is presented publicly as the way of keeping the peace and not offending

---

11. Rebecca Falconer, "Jeff Sessions escorted from Northwestern University amid protests," Axios, November 6, 2019, accessed November 18, 2019, http://www.axios.com/jeff-sessions-northwestern-university-protests-78b547f7-0a52-4bd5-81b3-b2ea6f54f826.html.

12. Madison Park and Kyung Lah, "Berkeley protests of Yiannopoulos caused $100,000 in damage," Axios, February 2, 2017, accessed November 18, 2019, http://www.cnn.com/2017/02/01/us/milo-yiannopoulos-berkeley/index.html.

13. Avery Anapol, "Jesuit university blocks Ben Shapiro event, saying it prompts 'hateful speech' from protesters," Hill, November 29, 2018, accessed November 18, 2019, https://thehill.com/blogs/blog-briefing-room/news/419025-jesuit-university-blocks-ben-shapiro-event-citing-hateful.

14. Hank Berrian, "Dave Rubin Says His Event Canceled Because Of Threats From Antifa," Daily Wire, September 26, 2019, accessed November 18, 2019, http://www.washingtonpost.com/news/volokh-conspiracy/wp/2016/02/25/cal-state-l-a-cancels-speech-by-conservative-writer-ben-shapiro/.

people but in actuality, it is the constriction of the freedom to express one's beliefs without fear of retribution.

Several colleges and universities have quarantined free speech by designating *free-speech zones*. These are often placed strategically in remote sections of campuses, away from more visible areas with the supposed intention of not stirring up violent reprisals among the students. One example of many such free-speech restrictions occurred at Arkansas State University (ASU). While an ASU student was setting up to get signatures for a local student-based, on-campus chapter of a national conservative organization, she was forcibly removed by the school's administration and campus law enforcement. A lawsuit began in early 2019 against the university,

> ASU now allows speeches and demonstrations in specified outdoor "free expression areas" between 8 a.m. and 9 p.m. Monday through Friday. The university policy states that 72 hours' notice is needed for requests to use other campus areas for such activities.
>
> The legal challenge to ASU comes from student Ashlyn Hoggard and a chapter of Turning Point USA, a conservative political group.
>
> Their lawsuit claims that in October 2017 an ASU official and a police officer ordered Hoggard and a representative of Turning Point USA, who had set up a recruiting table, to leave the campus's Heritage Plaza and stop speaking with students. The lawsuit states that a police officer "informed Ashlyn that she had violated the Student Conduct Code by engaging in speech outside of the speech zones."

The lawsuit alleges violation of the rights of freedom of speech and legal due process.[15]

In response to such actions that violate constitutional free speech, several states have assembled or enacted legislation prohibiting such rules. President Trump also signed an executive order to assure college students of the freedom of speech openly on campuses.[16]

This censorial atmosphere is often lauded as safeguarding innocent people. Though that may be the case to some degree, in the long run, it has only coddled and fomented a generation of fragile young people who are easily offended or hurt. Dave Rubin addressed this very problem in a transcript from a video segment on his show,

> Because of the authoritarian crusade to shelter young people from ideas that might challenge them, we've created safe spaces where once we had rigorous debate. We now issue trigger warnings where we once were brave enough to hear ideas that would make us uncomfortable. The attack on the honest debate

15. Jaime Adame, "Free-speech suit against ASU goes on despite new state law," *News, Arkansas Democrat Gazette*, February 25, 2019, accessed November 18, 2019, http://www.arkansasonline.com/news/2019/feb/25/free-speech-suit-against-asu-goes-on-de-1/.

16. Susan Syrluga, "Trump signs executive order on free speech on college campuses," Higher Education, Washington Post, March 21, 2019, accessed November 18, 2019, https://www.washingtonpost.com/education/2019/03/21/trump-expected-sign-executive-order-free-speech/.

has gotten so bad it is now hard to tell if this intellectual affliction is coming from the students or the faculty.[17]

Perhaps one of the most disconcerting examples of post-truth educational appropriation efforts gone awry is the Seattle school system's intention to teach mathematics, including intersectional and social justice banalities, as described in the Washington Free Beacon. In quoting from the Seattle Public Schools' own framework, the district wants to infuse addition, subtraction, et al. because it too has been "appropriated by Western culture" and used to "oppress and marginalize people and communities of color."[18] The same article goes on to reveal that,

> The proposed framework presents four themes for teachers to include in their K-12 math courses. The themes include how mathematical theories are "rooted in the ancient histories of people and empires of color," how contributions of communities of color to the field are ignored, and how learning math can be "an act of liberation."

17. Dave Rubin, "Let's Talk About Free Speech on Campus," The Direct Message, Rubin Report, February 25, 2016, accessed November18, 2019, http://www.ora.tv/rubinreport/2016/2/25/lets-talk-about-free-speech-on-campus.

18. Graham Piro, "Seattle Public Schools Considering Social Justice Math Curriculum," Issues, Washington Free Beacon, October 22, 2019, accessed October 22, 2019, http://freebeacon.com/issues/seattle-public-schools-considering-social-justice-math-curriculum/.

Students will ask introspective questions like "What is my mathematical identity?" "How does it feel to be a Mathematician?" and "What fears do we have about math?"

They will also consider issues of how important it is to be correct in studying mathematics. "How important is it to be Right? What is Right? Says Who?" one of the framework's proposed questions reads.[19]

Akin to the strategy of the postmodernists, the leadership of these aligned post-truth movements knows well that the best influential targets are education, politics, and the legal system. These institutions are the legs holding up our unique governing system and culture. Post-truth leaders will continue to contrive power to bring the world to where they want it, as every other errant ideology has done throughout history. It requires a core post-truth mentality that will disregard objective truth and seek to replace it with its own version in order to control outcomes in American society.

This strategic method of surreptitiously co-opting the influential foundational institutions of our American society has explicitly existed before post-truth came to be as it is today. Nevertheless, present-day post-truth movements have reached back into historical strategies of past nefarious dogmas to advance their agendas throughout critical areas of society. The central yet far-reaching tactic used over thirty years ago by the postmodernists has continued and been expanded by the hard-core post-truth idealists, in what is called *the long march through the institutions.*

19. Piro, *Seattle Public Schools Considering*, 14.

Roger Kimball in his book *The Long March: How the Cultural Revolution of the 1960s Changed America* made a searing observation about this tactic:

> In the Sixties and Seventies, after fantasies of overt political revolution faded, many student radicals urged their followers to undertake the "long march through the institutions." The phrase, popularized by the German New Leftist Rudi Dutschke, is often attributed to the Italian Marxist philosopher Antonio Gramsci—an unimpeachable authority for countercultural standard-bearers. But of course the phrase also carries the aura of an even higher authority: that of Mao Tse-tung and his long march and cultural revolution.
>
> In the context of Western societies, "the long march through the institutions" signified—in the words of Herbert Marcuse— "working against the established institutions while working in them." It was primarily by this means—by insinuation and infiltration rather than confrontation—that the countercultural dreams of radicals like Marcuse have triumphed. Bellbottoms, long hair, and incense were dispensable props; crucial was the hedonistic antinomianism they symbolized. In this sense, countercultural radicalism has come more and more to define the dominant culture even as the memory of student strikes and demonstrations fades under the distorting glaze of nostalgia.[20]

---

20. Roger Kimball, *The Long March: How the Cultural Revolution of the 1960s Changed America* (San Francisco: Encounter Books, 2000), 15.

This long march through the institutions comes with a price tag. The costly consequence of such extremism permeating American educational institutions was evidenced in the Evergreen College protests of 2017. Evergreen State College is an ultra-liberal and community-active college campus in Olympia, Washington. The college was having its annual *Day of Absence* and *Day of Presence.* Generally, on this day, minority students meet off-campus in workshops and discuss relevant social issues. This time all white people were asked to not come on campus instead. A professor by the name of Bret Weinstein sent an email to another professor, decrying the event as oppression itself and said he would be on campus that day regardless.

The email eventually leaked to the public, sparking a protest by some fifty students who confronted him outside his classroom, demanding he resign immediately. This action sparked further protests over the next two days, including confrontations with the police as well as a student-led interruption of a faculty meeting.[21] There were also reports of a group of students patrolling campus as a type of vigilante force carrying baseball bats, tasers, and batons.[22]

21. Bradford Richardson, "Students berate professor who refused to participate in no-whites 'Day of Absence,'"
https://m.washingtontimes.com/news/2017/may/25/evergreen-state-students-demand-professor-resign-f/, May 25, 2017, accessed October 15, 2019,
https://m.washingtontimes.com/news/2017/may/25/evergreen-state-students-demand-professor-resign-f/.

22. Jennifer Kabbany, "Students berate professor who refused to participate in no-whites 'Day of Absence,'" News, College Fix, June 5, 2017, accessed October 15,

The resemblance to what Ravi Zacarias termed as the hard meaning of post-truth[23] is astounding. The actual truth is ignored and derided. A new truth, as believed by a stronger majority, is forcibly imposed through various forms on others, even on those who are simply minding their own business.

The aggressive activism of post-truth-based ideologies is a natural result of the post-truth confusion and power struggle that ensues within the media and academy. These two unavoidably powerful influences on the mind and heart of the Western populace have had a significant role in forming post-truth chaos within the culture. Ravi Zacarias again instructs us well:

> Interestingly, the media, which flirt with untruths, and the academy, which never hesitates to replace absolutes with postmodern relativism, have come together to give our culture a new word. Their explanation is not so much that they are coining a new word as that they are affirming a reality—a truth about the way we coddle the lie, the ultimate self-defeating statement. It's a bit like another new phrase, "misremembering."
>
> We now live in a post-truth culture where misremembering is normal. (Not surprisingly, within hours of the American elections, a French television network baptized our culture as "post-logic.") These two bastions of values, the

2019, https://www.thecollegefix.com/evergreen-official-asks-student-vigilantes-stop-patrolling-campus-armed-bats-batons/.

23. Ravi Zacharias, "Why Oxford Dictionary's 2016 Word of the Year Matters," U.S. Edition, Gospel Coalition, December 21, 2016, accessed October 15, 2019, http://www.thegospelcoalition.org/article/why-oxford-dictionarys-2016-word-of-the-year-matters/.

academy and the media—where relativism flows in their veins—have become the town criers of this new word. Castigating the politicians, they untruthfully predicted the destination of the untruthful. Excoriating an electorate gone amuck, they wondered how people could be duped into a lie. Having themselves swallowed a camel, they strained a gnat. They are the primary carriers of word manipulation, repeating distortions often enough to make them into truths. Caring not for truth but for effect and for the manipulation of all thinking, their victory is pyrrhic.[24]

In the Scriptures, Paul the apostle is writing about the progression and acts of sinfulness in mankind, he says this in Romans 1:28-32:

> [28] And even as they did not like to retain God in *their* knowledge, God gave them over to a debased mind, to do those things which are not fitting; [29] being filled with all unrighteousness, sexual immorality, wickedness, covetousness, maliciousness; full of envy, murder, strife, deceit, evil-mindedness; *they are* whisperers, [30] backbiters, haters of God, violent, proud, boasters, inventors of evil things, disobedient to parents, [31] undiscerning, untrustworthy, unloving, unforgiving, unmerciful; [32] who, knowing the righteous judgment of God, that those who practice such things are deserving of death, not only do the same but also approve of those who practice them.

24. Zacarias, *Why Oxford Dictionary's 2016.*

Many of the characteristics of sinfulness in full bloom are in use in the extreme post-truth as a principled movement, as described by Paul in the previous paragraphs. The thinking is they cannot persuade you to accept their beliefs, so they use tactics of aggression, or even use violence, to either force conformity or remove opponents so they can better coalesce without being challenged.

Post-truth extremism is not a new collaboration of *inventors of evil things* (Rom. 1:30), but it is a modern refreshing of the old sinful tactic to *exchange the truth for a lie* (Rom. 1:25) and mislead thousands or millions to be convinced that their way is the only way to the real truth. We, as Christians especially, need to be vigilant of this (2 Tim. 4:2-5) by putting on the whole armor of God (Eph. 6:10-18), standing firm in the objective truth of God. We respond to false truth claims with the weaponry God has given us. That weaponry is not counter-aggression with harsh words, clubs, and baseball bats like the world, but, instead,the sword of the Spirit which is God's Word (Eph. 6:17) and the weapon of the love of Jesus Christ and His saving Gospel message (John 13:34-35, 15:13).

Chapter 8
Post-truth and Science

Today we live in what could be labeled the *scientific age*. By this, it is meant that science and scientists are regarded highly as the source for most of the answers to the questions mankind has. Many make the assertion that Christianity opposes and shuns science. This is both unfortunate and untrue.

Nevertheless, we also tend to believe science to be that one area where, due to its commitment to research and facts, it is assumed to be naturally untainted by any post-truth determinations. The reality is that post-truth permeates almost everything in life like an infectious virus, including science. Abdu Murray makes this same observation by saying: "My point is the post-truth virus is so powerful that it can infect all of us: politicians and voters, pastors and philosophers, soccer moms and baseball dads, and yes, even scientists."[1]

Notice in Murray's citation he does not say science. He accurately says *scientists*. We must always remember as apologist Frank Turek points out: "... science doesn't say anything, scientists do."[2] In other words, scientists are just as susceptible to all types of worldviews as anyone else regardless of their extensive knowledge and experience. In this era, it is the influence of post-truth that has infiltrated much of science as much as any, if not most, other fields of study. Murray helps put this reality into focus: "The creep of post-truth is seen in how we gather information about the world to conform to what we want to be true, not to what actually is true."[3]

Post-truth in science is manifested as *scientism*. It is not at all the same as actual science with its rigorous discipline of testing, observation, and conclusions deduced from the empirical data gathered. "Roughly, scientism is the view that the hard sciences—like chemistry, biology, physics, astronomy—provide the only genuine knowledge of reality."[4] Confusing scientism for science is intentional and orchestrated. Interestingly, there also are some shades of

---

1. Murray, *Saving Truth*, 16.
2. Frank Turek, *Stealing from God: Why Atheists Need God to Make Their Case* (Colorado Springs: NavPress, 2014), 146.
3. Murray, *Saving Truth*, 17.
4. J. P. Moreland, *Scientism and Secularism: Learning to Respond to a Dangerous Ideology* (Wheaton, IL: Crossway, 2018). Location 274.

difference in scientism as described by Christian philosopher J.P. Moreland:

> Strong scientism implies that something is true, rationally justified, or known if and only if it is a scientific claim that has been successfully tested and that is being used according to appropriate scientific methodology. There are no truths that can be known apart from appropriately certified scientific claims, especially those in the hard or natural sciences. ... Weak scientism is still scientism, but it allows for more "wiggle room." Weak scientism acknowledges truths apart from science, granting them some minimal rational status even if they don't have scientific support. Nevertheless, weak scientism still implies that science is by far the most authoritative sector of human knowing.[5]

Scientists are supposed to be concerned with the faithful interpretation of empirical facts that are repeatedly tested and observed. How could they be duped into accepting post-truth in place of the cold hard data and observable facts? The answer is that there are several areas of constant pressure which cause scientism to be the norm for scientists worldwide.

The first type of pressure we see is the religious-like commitment to two separate, but complementary, secular philosophies known as *naturalism* and *materialism*. The definition of naturalism is "a doctrine that denies a supernatural explanation of the origin or development of the universe and holds that scientific laws

5 Moreland, *Scientism and Secularism*, Location 330.

account for all of nature."[6] Materialism is defined as "a theory that everything can be explained as being or coming from matter."[7]

The tunnel vision of a materialism or naturalism-only based worldview willfully denies any admittance of possible theistic explanations (e.g., Creator God). "When you get down to the root of the problem, you find that the bad science of the Darwinists results from the false philosophy of naturalism or materialism at the foundation of their worldview."[8]

Most scientists start with the absolute and automatic rejection of any other possible explanation for the empirical data besides naturalism. "Everyone knows that theists have theological beliefs. However, few realize that atheistic scientists have theological beliefs as well. After all, "there is no God" and "life was not created by God" are theological beliefs."[9]

Scientism is sustained and protected by a form of intellectual elitism denying any theological or philosophical suggestions to bring answers to the questions. For any scientist to interject biblical suggestions for consideration is, by default, laughable. Moreland confirms this: "According to scientism, the claim that ethical and religious conclusions can be just as factual as science, and therefore

6. "Naturalism," *Merriam-Webster Dictionary*, accessed December 9, 2019, http://www.merriam-webster.com/dictionary/naturalism.

7. "Materialism," *Merriam-Webster Dictionary*, accessed December 9, 2019, https://www.merriam-webster.com/dictionary/materialism.

8. Geisler and Turek, *I Don't Have Enough*, 128.

9. Turek, *Stealing from God*, 172.

ought to be affirmed like scientific truths, may be a sign of bigotry and intolerance." [10]

The second type of pressure on those who practice scientism is financial. There is a limited pool of money (i.e., grants) upon which many scientists depend for their research, and the competition for those funds is intense. To obtain and hold on to the funding for their research many scientists fraudulently manipulate the data in order to justify the financial support of their work:

> This is the first meta-analysis of surveys asking scientists about their experiences of misconduct. It found that, on average, about 2% of scientists admitted to have fabricated, falsified or modified data or results at least once –a serious form of misconduct by any standard … and up to one third admitted a variety of other questionable research practices including "dropping data points based on a gut feeling", and "changing the design, methodology or results of a study in response to pressures from a funding source". In surveys asking about the behaviour of colleagues, fabrication, falsification and modification had been observed, on average, by over 14% of respondents, and other questionable practices by up to 72%. Over the years, the rate of admissions declined significantly in self-reports, but not in non-self-reports.[11]

10. Moreland, *Scientism and Secularism*, Location 267.

11. Daniele Fanelli, "How Many Scientists Fabricate and Falsify Research? A Systematic Review and Meta-Analysis of Survey Data," PLOS|ONE, May 29, 2009, accessed July, 2019, http://journals.plos.org/plosone/article?id=10.1371/journal.pone.0005738.

Abdu Murray comments on this monetary influence and peer pressure by saying, "In other words, the hard work of honest and forthright research is being undermined by the academic definition of success. No area is immune to post-truth infection."[12]

Perhaps the highest motivation for scientism is ideological. In other words, scientism does not approach things with an open mind to other possible explanations outside the natural realm. Its humanistic self-reliance, resting in their nest of vast knowledge and experience, must be preserved and protected. This area of the intelligentsia will not sacrifice status and tenure on the altar of what they consider utter foolishness (i.e., creationism). To elevate biblical fables to their level of academic knowledge is perceived as blasphemy. Conversely, if they were to allow just a cursory discussion of possibilities outside their hermetically sealed naturalistic world, they would be attacked by their own peers. Any hint of consideration of supernatural explanations would invite a torrent of formidable peer pressure, retaliation, and even rejection from the rest of the scientific community.

Probably there is no other overarching, worldwide example of scientism such as we see in the theories of evolution and man-made *global warming*. These two ideals are defended vigorously by a high number of scientists as not hypotheses but as a given fact. They believe these are facts agreed upon by consensus among almost all sensible scientists, not to be questioned or doubted.

12. Murray, *Saving Truth*, 17.

We first begin with an examination of global warming and climate change. NASA defines the two terms:

> What is global warming? Global warming refers to the long-term warming of the planet since the early 20th century, and most notably since the late 1970s, due to the increase in fossil fuel emissions since the Industrial Revolution. Worldwide since 1880, the average surface temperature has gone up by about 1 °C (about 2 °F), relative to the mid-20th-century baseline (of 1951-1980). This is on top of about an additional 0.15 °C of warming from between 1750 and 1880. What is climate change? Climate change refers to a broad range of global phenomena created predominantly by burning fossil fuels, which add heat-trapping gases to Earth's atmosphere. These phenomena include the increased temperature trends described by global warming, but also encompass changes such as sea level rise; ice mass loss in Greenland, Antarctica, the Arctic and mountain glaciers worldwide; shifts in flower/plant blooming; and extreme weather events.[13]

For years we have seen constant assertions from the media, government leaders, activist groups, scientists, and others demanding that man-made global warming be met with total commitment to its conclusions. They also believe then that immediate decisive and sweeping action be enacted by law before we and the planet are decimated. One of the countless examples of this alarmism is the

13. "What's in a name? Weather, global warming and climate change," climate.nasa.gov, accessed August 8, 2019, https://climate.nasa.gov/resources/global-warming/.

recent call for an immediate emergency declaration and response of massive resources by Senator Bernie Sanders and Representative Alexandria Ocasio-Cortez.[14] The alarmist politicization of global warming further reveals the true identity of this movement not as a clarion call to respond to genuinely undeniable empirical data but instead as post-truth scientism at a fever-pitch level.

Urgent pleas for immediate and sweeping worldwide reaction to similarly manufactured catastrophes have occurred before in various forms in the 1970s, 80s, and 90s.[15] They too were based on the apparent near-unanimous consensus of scientists worldwide. These past impending calamities include the new ice age, acid rain,[16] and the ever-widening hole in the ozone layer[17] unleashing

14. Kristoffer Tigue, "AOC, Sanders Call for 'Climate Emergency' Declaration in Congress," inside climate news, July 10, 2019, accessed August 8, 2019, http://insideclimatenews.org/news/09072019/sanders-aoc-ocasio-cortez-climate-change-emergency-declaration-congress-washington-flooding.

15. Anthony Watts, "The 1970's Global Cooling Compilation – looks much like today," Watts Up With That?, March 1, 2013, accessed August 12, 2019, http://wattsupwiththat.com/2013/03/01/global-cooling-compilation/.

16. John P. Rafferty, "What Happened to Acid Rain?," ENCYCLOPÆDIA BRITANNICA, accessed August 12, 2019, https://www.britannica.com/story/what-happened-to-acid-rain.

17. Erin Blakemore, "The Ozone Hole Was Super Scary, What Happened To It?," smithsonian.com, January 13, 2016, accessed August 12, 2019, https://www.smithsonianmag.com/science-nature/ozone-hole-was-super-scary-what-happened-it-180957775/.

astronomical radiation levels of the sun because of chlorofluorocarbons (CFCs) in the aerosol cans we used.[18]

The reality is there were – and are – legitimate concerns on particular challenges or threats to our environment and health that can be backed by information from credible sources needing a carefully measured and effective response. Yet with man-made global warming, it is fabricated in post-truth, which bypasses and disallows any consideration of valid contrary information from credible sources. Instead, it only offers *ad hominem*[19] arguments and attacks, thus shielding the masses from weighing the evidence from all sides of the issue and coming to their own conclusions. Global warming has the veneer of mounds of evidence belied by its commitment to its preconceived beliefs, politicization, and religious devotion to the cause.

The global warming movement has had roots since the 1970s in European-based Marxist and socialist beliefs and political activism in the 1970s. It started in Sweden, then spread to Germany, and finally into the United States. Rupert Darwall, a corporate strategist and a board director of Reform, a London-based think tank, summarizes this in his book *Green Tyranny*: "For Europe's green

18. Nicholas Thomspon, "Nuclear War and Nuclear Fear in the 1970's and 1980's," *Journal of Contemporary History* 46, no. 1 (2011).

19. "Ad Hominem," *Merriam-Webster Dictionary*, accessed December 16, 2019, https://www.merriam-webster.com/dictionary/ad%20hominem. Definition of ad hominem,1: appealing to feelings or prejudices rather than intellect, 2: marked by or being an attack on an opponent's character rather than by an answer to the contentions made.

radicals, control of energy policy is a means toward an end. Global warming thus poses a question about the nature and purpose of the state: whether its role is to effect a radical transformation of society or whether its principal task is to protect freedom."[20]

An example of the large-scale tilt to just such superiority is seen in the false assumptions and accusations that *climate deniers* insulate themselves and their adherents from the real evidence, and are nothing more than extremists:

> It is not simply that climate-change deniers don't believe in facts, it's that they only want to accept those facts that justify their ideology. Like all conspiracy theorists, they feel entitled to a double standard whereby they simultaneously believe (with no evidence) that the world's climate scientists are part of a global conspiracy to hype the evidence on climate change, but then cherry pick the most favorable scientific statistics that allegedly show that the global temperature has not gone up in the last two decades. Deniers and other ideologues routinely embrace an obscenely high standard of doubt toward facts that they don't want to believe, alongside complete credulity toward any facts that fit with their agenda. The main criterion is what favors their preexisting beliefs. This is not the abandonment of facts, but a corruption of the process by which facts are credibly gathered and reliably used to shape one's beliefs about reality. Indeed, the rejection of this undermines the idea that some things are true irrespective of how we feel about them, and that it is in our best

---

20. Rupert Darwall, *Green Tyranny: Exposing the Totalitarian Roots of the Climate Industrial Complex* (New York: Encounter Books, 2017), xvi.

interests (and those of our policy makers) to attempt to find them.[21]

Of course, global warming devotees are never guilty of the same charge, thus proving our point of post-truth influence in science today. It reflects the hard meaning of post-truth as described earlier by Ravi Zacarias by intentionally presenting something verifiably incorrect in order to fulfill the predetermined goal.

One of the most condemning and discrediting blows to the climate change movement of the 2000s was what became known as *Climategate*. On two separate occasions, online hackers broke into the computer servers of climate research facilities, exposing the discussions of climate scientists and their manipulations of data to align with the pre-conceived narrative of man-made global warming.[22] The first instance of this revelation to the public was the aforementioned original Climategate, and the second was referred to popularly as Climategate 2.0.[23]

To be clear, it must be understood that scientists cannot be expected to be entirely neutral, but they can be expected to be

21. McIntyre, *Post-Truth*, Location 230.

22. Juliet Eilperin, "Hackers steal electronic data from top climate research center," *Washington Post*, November 1, 2009, accessed August 12, 2019, http://www.washingtonpost.com/wp-dyn/content/article/2009/11/20/AR2009112004093.html.

23. James Taylor, "Climategate 2.0: New E-Mails Rock The Global Warming Debate," Forbes, November 23, 2011, accessed August 12, 2019, http://www.washingtonpost.com/wp-dyn/content/article/2009/11/20/AR2009112004093.html.

intellectually honest with themselves and the facts. The reason for this is not always sinister or deceptive. Scientists have to assume certain philosophical ideals or principles as any other person to be able to make clear and reasonable judgments from the evidence gathered. Dr. Frank Turek, in his book *Stealing from God*, helps us to understand this:

> Before doing science: Scientists frame their own philosophical rules for doing science. For example, should scientists be open to only natural causes, or are intelligent causes possible? How about supernatural causes? Those questions can't be answered by science; they are answered by scientists doing philosophy. While doing science: Scientists rely on the orderly laws of nature, the law of causality, and the theory of knowledge known as realism when conducting an experiment or historical investigation. After doing science: Scientists must decide what is good evidence. What counts as evidence is not evidence itself—a philosophical value judgment must be made. Scientists must then interpret the evidence they've judged to be good by relying on all the immaterial realities listed above to draw a free and rational conclusion. They must also be honest throughout the entire process.[24]

J.P. Moreland, in his book *Scientism and Secularism,* explains that philosophical thought is a natural and necessary part of science, calling it *first philosophy*:

24. Turek, *Stealing from God*, 165.

What, exactly, is first philosophy? Roughly, first philosophy is the notion that there is a realm of rational investigation that (1) is the proper domain of philosophy, (2) is independent of and, indeed, more basic or fundamental than science (that is, science is built upon the foundation of the results of first philosophy), and (3) gives us knowledge of the topics studied in that realm, including knowledge of reality.[25]

To reinforce the understanding of the necessity of philosophy as a foundation for formulating scientific opinions or conclusions, Moreland includes this quote from French philosopher and scholar Étienne Gilson, in his book *The Unity of Philosophical Experience*, who said, "Philosophy is the only rational knowledge by which both science and nature can be judged. By reducing philosophy to pure science, man has...abdicated his right to judge nature."[26] This acceptance and understanding of basic philosophical tenets in approaching the scientific process and data is now being substituted by scientism. This is done by the same scientism that doggedly forces conclusions through a limited scope of philosophical beliefs and presuppositions.

Another area of scientism that has had the most enduring impact in academia, science, and education is the theory of *evolution*. The argument to be discussed here is not with presenting the theory's arguments themselves, but of the evidence and attitude of scientism

---

25. Moreland, *Scientism and Secularism*, Location 1460.
26. Moreland, *Scientism and Secularism*. quoted in Étienne Gilson, The Unity of Philosophical Experience (New York: Charles Scribner's Sons, 1937), 223.

among evolutionary-based scientists as being the *only* possible way all life forms have come into existence and developed over time.

Frank Turek and the late Normal Geisler, two of the leading apologists of the Christian faith wrote about the weakness of scientism:

> Finally, many modern intellectuals imply that any box top based on religion wouldn't be legitimate anyway. Why? Because, they say, only science yields truth. Not only has evolution removed the need for God, they say, but only what is testable in a laboratory can be considered true. That is, only science deals in matters of fact, while religion stays merely in the realm of faith. So there's no sense trying to muster evidence or facts to support religion, because that would be like mustering facts to prove that chocolate ice cream tastes better than vanilla ice cream. You can't prove preferences. Therefore, since they insist that religion is never a matter of objective fact but merely subjective taste, any box top derived from religion couldn't provide the objective picture of life we're looking for.[27]

Richard Dawkins, perhaps the most prominent of the leading new atheists in recent years, makes this remark in his book *The Blind Watchmaker*: "Biology is the study of complicated things that give the appearance of having been designed for a purpose."[28] In his elaboration of the complexities and accuracies of nature, he goes to

27. Norman L. Geisler and Frank Turek, *I Don't Have Enough Faith to Be an Atheist* (Wheaton, IL: Crossway, 2004), 21.

28. Richard Dawkins, *The Blind Watchmaker* (New York: W.W. Nortonamp and Company,, 1987), 3.

the intelligent design argument of William Paley's watch as proof of an intelligent watchmaker. Nevertheless, Dawkins denies this is evidence of any Creator-God but redefines the watchmaker in this way:

> The analogy between telescope and eye, between watch and living organism, is false. All appearances to the contrary, the only watchmaker in nature is the blind forces of physics, albeit deployed in a very special way. A true watchmaker has foresight: he designs his cogs and springs, and plans their interconnections, with a future purpose in his mind's eye. Natural selection, the blind, unconscious, automatic process which Darwin discovered, and which we now know is the explanation for the existence and apparently purposeful form of all life, has no purpose in mind. It has no mind and no mind's eye. It does not plan for the future. It has no vision, no foresight, no sight at all. If it can be said to play the role of watchmaker in nature, it is the blind watchmaker.[29]

This is a primary example of post-truth as scientism. The evolutionist will remain with his presupposed naturalism-only framework and filter out all hypotheses that do not come from that framework. This is akin to the aforementioned *confirmation bias,* which is the reinforcement of one's beliefs by only going to sources that will support the desired viewpoint.

Another term used to describe evolution is a subset of scientism named *evolutionism.* Evolutionism is defined as "a belief in the

29. Dawkins, *The Blind Watchmaker*, 9.

concept of evolution as an explanation for most—if not all—details of the universe."[30] Evolutionists decry it as a gimmicky, derogatory word invented and used by creationists. Michael Ruse, a professor of philosophy at Florida State University and an atheist, wrote concerning this,

> A major complaint of the Creationists, those who are committed to a Genesis-based story of origins, is that evolution—and Darwinism in particular—is more than just a scientific theory. They object that too often evolution operates as a kind of secular religion, pushing norms and proposals for proper (or, in their opinion, improper) action. Evolutionists dismiss this argument as merely another rhetorical debating trick, and in major respects, this is precisely what it is. It is silly to claim that a naturalistic story of origins leads straight to sexual freedom and other supposed ills of modern society. But, if we wish to deny that evolution is more than just a scientific theory, the Creationists do have a point.[31]

Later in the same article, Ruse admits, "I am saying that this popular evolutionism—often an alternative to religion—exists."[32] Mike Riddle, Founder and President of Creation Training Initiative, an Apologist and Education Specialist, responding to the writer of

---

30. "What is evolutionism?," Got Questions Ministries, accessed December 11, 2019, https://www.gotquestions.org/evolutionism.html.

31. Michael Ruse, "Is Evolution a Secular Religion?," *Science* 299, no. 5612 (March 2003): 1523, accessed December 11, 2019, http://dx.doi.org/10.1126/science.1082968.

32. Ruse, "Is Evolution a Secular," 1524.

this project, explains his use of the term evolutionism: "I do so to relegate it to a philosophical explanation rather than a scientific explanation. I feel justified in doing so because there is no observable evidence to support "true" evolution – amoeba to man." (Email to Mike Riddle, Evolution defined - request for Mike, 2019)

The problem with scientism is that actual science is systemically (and correctly) based on gathering evidence, repeated testing, and observation upon which the scientist arrives at reasonable, good-faith conclusions – even if it disproves their presuppositions. That is science, not scientism. Unfortunately, in our post-truth society, scientism is actually what is promoted, repeated, and blindly adhered to under the guise of its supposed "consensus."[33]

---

33. Yehoshua Socol, Yair Y. Shaki, and Moshe Yanovskiy, "Interests, Bias, and Consensus in Science and Regulation," Sage Journals, June 5, 2019, accessed October 21, 2019, http://doi.org/10.1177/1559325819853669.

Chapter 9

Post-truth and Corporate America

One of the most powerful representations of the influence of post-truth-based ideals such as intersectionality and social justice is displayed in corporate America. The vociferous public (and monetary) protest by companies aimed at individuals, communities, cities, and states goes under the description of *virtue signaling*. The dictionary definition of virtue signaling states it is "an attempt to show other people that you are a good person, for example by expressing opinions that will be acceptable to them, especially on social media."[1] A more descriptive definition of it is "the practice of

1. "Virtue Signaling," accessed October 22, 2019,

    http://dictionary.cambridge.org/us/dictionary/english/virtue-signalling.

trying to put one's own moral superiority on display by saying or doing something that has no real practical benefit other than to announce agreement with the most stylish opinion of whatever happens to be trending at the moment."[2]

The corporate entities, both large and small, that practice virtue signaling have increased in number and are willing participants competing to outshine one another in the public domain of those who consume their products and services. They carry the banner of the current far-left (post-truth based) diatribes in order to appear sensitive to the inadequacies and injustices committed by and against so many in our society. They propose themselves as game changers in helping to right the wrongs that pervade the culture.

Perhaps the most significant example of this is seen in the controversial incident referred to as the *Google Memo*. One of Google's employees, engineer James Demore, originally sent an internal memo to others entitled *Google's Ideological Echo Chamber*. He wrote it after he attended one of the company's diversity training sessions and was subsequently fired by the company. The amplification of what goes on inside Google came as a result of his attendance at one of the company's diversity training sessions, which

2. James Manning, "Virtue Signaling: The New Evangelistic Strategy | Phil Johnson," Sovereign Nations, January 30, 2019, accessed October 24, 2019, https://sovereignnations.com/2019/01/30/virtue-signaling-new-evangelistic-strategy-phil-johnson/#kScwCVcxDMVtgxt8.99.

he described as "secretive" and "shameful." [3] Nevertheless, his email expressed a sound factual explanation with evidence and helpful suggestions to improve the situation and not to demean or tear down women or anyone else. His unpardonable sin was to dare express factual and empirically verified truth amid the subjective post-truth judges of political correctness.[4]

Demore's inside email eventually leaked to the public, where he was eviscerated on social media and other media outlets, as well as supported by many. The controversy swirls around his comments where he stated, among other things, that:

> ...the male-female gap in employment at Google may not be entirely the result of discrimination against women, although he explicitly acknowledges that some female engineers may face discriminatory barriers.
>
> The memo includes such crimethink nuggets as "women, on average, have... a stronger interest in people rather than things, relative to men," and that men have a "higher drive for status." ... He even goes on to suggest ways Google could make its culture more appealing to women without forced, affirmative action-style diversity programs, such as trying to make software engineering jobs more collaborative and people-oriented.[5]

3. Shona Gosh, "The fired Google engineer wrote his memo after he went to a 'shaming,' 'secretive' diversity program," Business Insider, August 9, 2017, accessed October 22, 2019,

4. Inez Feltscher Stepman, *Google Fires Engineer For*, 14.

5. Inez Feltscher Stepman, "Google Fires Engineer For Noticing Men And Women Are Different," Federalist, August 8, 2017, accessed October 22, 2019,

Damore continued to face vociferous shaming from countless far-left post-truth activists. During a panel discussion at Portland State University, the militant leftist group Antifa made threats and posted flyers before the event to incite protesters.[6] During the event, an audience member interrupted by screaming the panel was not diverse enough. This was followed by others smashing the sound equipment, rendering the microphones useless, though the guests and hosts were undeterred and continued speaking, just the same.[7]

Since his dismissal, Demore has been the core of a class-action lawsuit filed against Google for bias and discrimination based on gender, race, and political bias. A judge upheld that the case could proceed against the objections by Google as to its validity.[8]

In 2015, Angie's List pulled out of an agreement with the city of Indianapolis and with the state of Indiana, nixing a new headquarters expansion there.[9] The reason? They disagreed with the

http://thefederalist.com/2017/08/08/google-fires-engineer-noticing-men-women-different/.

6. Lauren Cooley, "Activists smash sound equipment at 'Google memo' author's university talk," Washington Examiner, February 19, 2018, accessed October 24, 2019, http://www.washingtonexaminer.com/activists-smash-sound-equipment-at-google-memo-authors-university-talk.

7. Cooley, *Activists Smash Sound Equipment.*

8. Anna Hopkins, "Judge rules lawsuit accusing Google of bias against conservatives can proceed," Big Tech Backlash, Fox News, June 10, 2019, accessed October 22, 2019, http://www.foxnews.com/tech/google-conservative-bias-case-james-damore.

9. Jeff Swiatek, "Angie's List nixes Indy deal over 'religious freedom' law," Money, USA Today, March 28, 2015, accessed October 24, 2019,

state's new Religious Freedom law. The legislation, approved by Indiana's GOP-controlled House and Senate, prevents state and local governments from "substantially burdening" a person's exercise of religion unless a compelling governmental interest can be proved."[10] Then-Governor Pence signed it into law.[11] Afterward, under intense political pressure, Pence then signed a weaker version of the law.[12]

In 2017, the NBA pulled the All-Star game out of Charlotte, North Carolina, in protest of the city of Charlotte and the state's new law requiring transgender people to use the bathroom according to their gender assigned to them at birth. Soon after, under the tremendous corporate monetary pressure, the state capitulated and rescinded that law. Due to the repeal, the NBA restored the game to Charlotte.[13]

https://www.usatoday.com/story/money/business/2015/03/28/angies-list-cancels-indy-expansion-religious-freedom-law/70598270/.

10. Jeff Swiatek, "Indiana's Governor Signs 'Religious Freedom' Bill," America, NPR, March 26, 2015, accessed October 24, 2019, https://www.npr.org/sections/thetwo-way/2015/03/26/395583706/indianas-governor-signs-religious-freedom-bill.

11. Swiatek, *Indiana's Governor Signs 'Religious*.

12. Rebecca Kaplan, "Indiana's Governor Signs 'Religious Freedom' Bill," News, CBS News, April 2, 2015, accessed October 24, 2019, https://www.cbsnews.com/news/indiana-lawmakers-announce-deal-to-update-religious-freedom-law/.

13. Daniel Trotta, "NBA returns all-star game to N. Carolina after transgender law lifted," Sports News, Reuters, May 24, 2017, accessed October 24, 2019, http://www.reuters.com/article/us-usa-lgbt-nba/nba-returns-all-star-game-to-north-carolina-after-transgender-law-lifted-idUSKBN18K26W.

Perhaps one of the perpetual examples of virtue signaling has been perpetuated on Chick-Fil-A after the CEO, Dan Cathy, made statements regarding his support for the traditional marriage of one man, one woman:

> Some have opposed the company's support of the traditional family. "Well, guilty as charged," said Cathy when asked about the company's position.
>
> "We are very much supportive of the family -- the biblical definition of the family unit. We are a family-owned business, a family-led business, and we are married to our first wives. We give God thanks for that.
>
> "We operate as a family business ... our restaurants are typically led by families; some are single. We want to do anything we possibly can to strengthen families. We are very much committed to that," Cathy emphasized.
>
> "We intend to stay the course," he said. "We know that it might not be popular with everyone, but thank the Lord, we live in a country where we can share our values and operate on biblical principles."[14]

Years after those comments, censorship, and exclusion of the nation's third-largest restaurant chain have included Rider

---

14. K. Allan Blume, "'Guilty as charged,' Cathy says of Chick-fil-A's stand on biblical & family values," News, Baptist Press, July 16, 2012, accessed December 26, 2019, http://www.bpnews.net/38271.

University,[15] San Antonio International Airport[16], and a Tampa school which rejected the free lunch offered by the local Chick-fil-A.[17]

A few of those in corporate leadership are true believers in helping to shape a better society for all people, yet it becomes evident that the moral gerrymandering of virtue signaling is about the bottom line. In reality, it is a marketing tool exploited to attract more customers and increase profits. Family Research Council media coordinator Joshua Arnold remarks, "In exploiting today's dominant rhetoric on contentious social issues, it's almost as if big businesses are like actors playing a part, poorly hiding their true profit motive behind a mask."[18] Ironically it more often alienates more potential

15. Jessica Chasmar, "Rider University rejects Chick-fil-A as students' top pick for new eatery, citing 'corporate values,'" *Culture Clash, Washington Times,* November 22, 2018, accessed October 24, 2019, http://www.washingtontimes.com/news/2018/nov/22/rider-university-rejects-chick-fil-a-as-students-t/.

16. Kelly Tyko, "San Antonio council rejects proposal to reconsider Chick-fil-A at Texas airport," Money, USA Today, April 18, 2019, accessed October 24, 2019, https://www.usatoday.com/story/money/2019/04/18/chick-fil-ban-texas-council-rejects-proposal-reconsider-location/3508448002/.

17. WWWLTV.com, "Lusher High School turns down free Chick-fil-A lunch 'out of respect to our LGBTQ staff,'" Local, 4WWL, October 10, 2019, accessed October 24, 2019, https://www.wwltv.com/article/news/local/lusher-high-school-turns-down-free-chick-fil-a-lunch-over-companys-anti-lgbtq-history/289-70b1156b-2c39-4285-9692-1d186d161594.

18. Joshua Arnold, "Big business virtue signaling is bombing with consumers," Opinion, Washington Examiner, August 2, 2019, accessed October 28, 2019, https://www.washingtonexaminer.com/opinion/op-eds/big-business-virtue-signaling-is-bombing-with-consumers.

customers than gains new and additional ones, yet the businesses persist. Arnold backs this up with the evidence:

> Big business has failed spectacularly in its gambit to boost its credibility through taking far-left policy stances. Another nationwide opinion poll by Gallup shows public confidence in big business in 2019 (as opposed to all business leaders measured in the Pew poll) is at 23% — about where it was in 2003.
>
> Why hasn't their tactic worked? Because people can smell a phony. Big business isn't winning any friends with their rampant hypocrisy.
>
> They've just alienated social conservatives by swallowing the rhetoric of the abortion and LGBT lobbies hook, line, and sinker.[19]

Herein openly lies a strategy to influence people to come into conformity with the current groupthink's ultimate truth claims but with the added motive of monetary gain.

19. Arnold, *Big Business Virtue Signaling.*

Chapter 10

Post-truth Dogmata

Post-truth does not announce itself as such. It is the system and thinking behind several new ideologies or ones borrowing from the pre-modern and modern periods, respectively. It is an expression originally rooted in postmodernism but is now expressing itself in contemporary society through several competing popular ideologies that we will describe briefly. Following this chapter, we will discuss the core fallacies and failures of the leading post-truth systems.

What then are the primary ideologies that are seeping into society from the academy and the media and thrust into the establishments in which we engage daily? What current mainline, post-truth generated ideas are causing language and cultural change to the point of causing growing confusion and provoking extreme polarization and even violence?

As mentioned before, post-truth has quickly emerged ahead of its parent theory, postmodernism, to become the fundamental paradigm for education, politics, the media, and activism. In the vacuum created by ignoring objective truth, it is open-range time for any self-created ideas to compete for the majority groupthink that will fill that void. It has now opened a virtual Pandora's Box by providing the basic elemental parts to be used together by anyone to form a stand-alone theory of thought and practice. It indeed has now produced what Abdu Murray calls the *Culture of Confusion*.[1]

In the following sections, we will explore the most ubiquitous areas of post-truth-based belief systems that often overlap and are vying for ultimate control of the hearts and minds of people. This will be followed by a more precise understanding and critique of the true nature of such ideas.

Intersectionality

Perhaps the predominant and most well-established belief system steering the majority of our culture's thinking and behavior is called *intersectionality*. It is defined by Lexico, an Oxford dictionary online resource: "The interconnected nature of social categorizations such as race, class, and gender, as they apply to a given individual or group, regarded as creating overlapping and interdependent systems

1. Murray, *Saving Truth*, 23.

of discrimination or disadvantage."[2] In other words, a person is not discriminated against by race alone but also by any growing number of social, physical, sexual, and economic categories.

Educators and authors such as Peggy McIntosh, in her classic piece *White Privilege: Unpacking the Invisible Knapsack*[3], Bell Hooks, in her landmark work *Teaching to Transgress,*[4] and Kimberlé Crenshaw are some of the founders of the theory of Intersectionality. It arose from the nascent feminist theory or studies of the 1970s and 1980s taught in the humanities and social sciences departments of the academy in America.

The term Intersectionality became popularized due to two critical essays written by Kimberlé Crenshaw, a civil rights activist and legal scholar: *Demarginalizing the Intersection of Race and Sex: A Black Feminist Critique of Antidiscrimination Doctrine, Feminist Theory and Antiracist Politics* (1989), and *Mapping the Margins: Intersectionality, Identity Politics, and Violence against Women of Color* (1991).

In her first breakout paper in 1989, written for the University of Chicago Legal Forum, Crenshaw wrote, "traditional feminist ideas and antiracist policies exclude black women because they face

2. Lexico, "s.v. Intersectionality," accessed October 7, 2019,
   http://www.lexico.com/en/definition/intersectionality.

3. P. McIntosh, "White Privilege: Unpacking the Invisible Knapsack.," *Peace and Freedom* (July/August 1989), under "Pages 10–12."

4. Bell Hooks, *Teaching to Transgress: Education as the Practice of Freedom* (New York: Routledge, 1994).

overlapping discrimination unique to them."[5] Crenshaw illustrated it in this way:

> Consider an analogy to traffic in an intersection, coming and going in all four directions. Discrimination, like traffic through an intersection, may flow in one direction, and it may flow in another. If an accident happens in an intersection, it can be caused by cars traveling from any number of directions and, sometimes, from all of them. Similarly, if a Black woman is harmed because she is in the intersection, her injury could result from sex discrimination or race discrimination.[6]

In other words, Crenshaw is saying that a black woman does not experience discrimination for only being black or only as a woman, independently of each other. The two characteristics intersect and raise the degree of discrimination against them.

This theory of social hierarchy, as constructed by Crenshaw, quickly expanded into a big-tent designation, including any number of categories not even considered in the 1980s and 1990s, including sexuality, gender, ability, age, and other identity-based categories. Even Crenshaw, in an interview before the twentieth anniversary of the African American Policy Forum, gave a somewhat arm's-length

---

5. Merrill Perlman, "The origin of the term 'intersectionality'," Language Corner, Columbia Journalism Review, October 23, 2018, accessed October 7, 2019, https://www.cjr.org/language_corner/intersectionality.php.

6. Kimberlé Crenshaw, "Demarginalizing the Intersection of Race and Sex: A Black Feminist Critique of Antidiscrimination Doctrine, Feminist Theory and Antiracist Politics," *University of Chicago Legal Forum* 1989, no. 1: 149.

description of intersectionality as being much broader than originally intended:

> Some people look to intersectionality as a grand theory of everything, but that's not my intention. If someone is trying to think about how to explain to the courts why they should not dismiss a case made by black women, just because the employer did hire blacks who were men and women who were white, well, that's what the tool was designed to do. If it works, great. If it doesn't work, it's not like you have to use this concept. The other issue is that intersectionality can get used as a blanket term to mean, "Well, it's complicated."[7]

Intersectionality has expanded in the twenty years since Crenshaw's inception of the concept and term. Patricia Hill Collins and Sirma Bilge in their book *Intersectionality* (2016) have described this in detail:

> Intersectionality is a way of understanding and analyzing the complexity in the world, in people, and in human experiences. The events and conditions of social and political life and the self can seldom be understood as shaped by one factor. They are generally shaped by many factors in diverse and mutually influencing ways. When it comes to social inequality, people's lives and the organization of power in a given society are better understood as being shaped not by a single axis of social division,

7. "Kimberlé Crenshaw on Intersectionality, More than Two Decades Later," Latest
News, Columbia Law School, June 8, 2017, accessed October 7, 2019,
https://www.law.columbia.edu/pt-br/news/2017/06/kimberle-crenshaw-
intersectionality.

be it race or gender or class, but by many axes that work together and influence each other. Intersectionality as an analytic tool gives people better access to the complexity of the world and of themselves.[8]

Professors Grace Ji-Sun Kim and Susan M. Shaw in their book *Intersectional Theology* explain it in more concise language,

> Intersectionality is the recognition of the simultaneity of multiple social identities within interlocking systems of oppression— people experience always and at once their gender, race, sexual identity, ability, age, social class, nation, and religion, and those intertwined identities locate them in relation to structures of power and domination.[9]

Intersectionality is often considered to be an outgrowth of what is called *Critical race theory*. "*Critical race theory (*CRT), the view that race, instead of being biologically grounded and natural, is socially constructed and that race, as a socially constructed concept, functions as a means to maintain the interests of the white population that constructed it."[10] In her book *Intersectionality as Critical Social Theory*, Patricia Hill Collins calls intersectionality ". . . a critical social theory

8. Patricia Hill Collins, and Sirma Bilge, *Intersectionality*, 2nd ed., Key concepts (Medford, MA: Polity Press, 2020), 5.

9. Grace Ji-Sun Kim, and Susan M. Shaw, "Biography as Intersectional Theology," in *Intersectional Theology: An Introductory Guide*, kindle ed. (Minneapolis, MN: Fortress Press, 2018), Location 240.

10. Tommy Curry, "Critical race theory," Social Sciences, Encyclopedia Britannica, accessed October 29, 2019, http://www.britannica.com/topic/critical-race-theory.

in the making."[11] Critical race theory (CRT) had its beginnings in the 1970s and grew from there in writing and publication, importance, and influence.

> Critical race theory sprang up in the mid-1970s, as a number of lawyers, activists, and legal scholars across the country realized, more or less simultaneously, that the heady advances of the civil rights era of the 1960s had stalled and, in many respects, were being rolled back. Realizing that new theories and strategies were needed to combat the subtler forms of racism that were gaining ground, early writers such as Derrick Bell, Alan Freeman, and Richard Delgado (coauthor of this primer) put their minds to the task. They were soon joined by others, and the group held its first conference at a convent outside Madison, Wisconsin, in the summer of 1989.[12]

There are some key buzzwords used within critical race theory and intersectionality that need to be mentioned and recognized. These terms (like intersectionality and social justice) have varied meanings depending on who is defining them, and at what time period.

Woke is one of the ideology's most used terms referring to someone aware of the social inequalities, especially of African Americans:

---

11. Patricia Hill Collins, *Intersectionality as Critical Social Theory*, kindle ed. (Durham: Duke University Press, 2019), Location 274.
12. Richard Delgado and Jean Stefancic, *Critical race theory: An Introduction* (New York: New York University Press, 2001), 3–4.

Stay woke became a watch word in parts of the black community for those who were self-aware, questioning the dominant paradigm and striving for something better. But *stay woke* and *woke* became part of a wider discussion in 2014, immediately following the shooting of Michael Brown in Ferguson, Missouri. The word *woke* became entwined with the Black Lives Matter movement; instead of just being a word that signaled awareness of injustice or racial tension, it became a word of action. Activists were *woke* and called on others to *stay woke*.[13]

White Privilege is a foundational and frequently used phrase by these racial-based theories, and it "Refers to the unquestioned and unearned set of advantages, entitlements, benefits and choices bestowed on people solely because they are white. Generally white people who experience such privilege do so without being conscious of it."[14]

A related term to white privilege also used by critical race theory, and related theories, is that of *white fragility*. Leading author on the subject Dr. Robin DiAngelo defines it:

White Fragility is a state in which even a minimum amount of racial stress becomes intolerable, triggering a range of defensive

13. "Stay Woke: The new sense of 'woke' is gaining popularity," Words We're Watching, Merriam-Webster, September, 2017, accessed November 19, 2019, https://www.merriam-webster.com/words-at-play/woke-meaning-origin.

14. "White fragility: why it's so hard for white people to talk about racism," White Privilege, Racial Equity Tools, October, 2019, accessed November 19, 2019, https://www.racialequitytools.org/resourcefiles/RET_Glossary_Updated_October_2019_.pdf.

moves. These moves include the outward display of emotions such as anger, fear, and guilt, and behaviors such as argumentation, silence, and leaving the stress-inducing situation.[15]

The difficulties of the false assumptions - and presumptions – of critical race theory abound when laid against the backdrop of reality and empirical observations of humanity, and mainly when laid against the Word of God:

Following Bell and Crenshaw, critical race theory often operates like a conspiracy theory in which there are few, if any, intentional conspirators. Instead, we are all unwittingly complicit in the "sins" of racial bigotry that are presumed to be immanent, permanent, and ordinary, especially in American society. This includes a denial of significant progress on these issues throughout history, claiming instead that racial problems, including white supremacy, do not so much get overcome as they learn to wear more subtle and nicer-looking masks. This, for instance, is often buttressed by Bell's "Interest-Convergence Thesis," which indicates that dominant groups (here: whites) only ever extend increased rights, liberties, and equality to disenfranchised minority groups when it is in the best interests of the dominant groups to do so. That is, under Bell's thesis, racial issues do not improve; white supremacy merely finds a

---

15. Robin DiAngelo, "White Fragility," *International Journal of Critical Pedagogy* 3, no. 3 (2011), accessed November 11, 2019, http://libjournal.uncg.edu/ijcp/article/viewFile/249/116.

comelier way to present itself in seeming while it continues mostly unabated.[16]

Oppressed v. the Oppressor

Deeply embedded in the theoretical framework of intersectionality and critical race theory is the notion that based on any number of intersecting types of categories in which you fall, you are either an *oppressor* of others or the oppressed *victim* of others. There is no real middle ground, regardless of the clear and great amount of evidence indicating a person has never been discriminatory against anyone, for any reason at all, for their entire life. This is acutely illustrated in Figure 1.

16. James Lindsay, "The Trojan Horse Episode 3: Critical race theory," Sovereign Nations, October 11, 2019, accessed October 29, 2019, https://sovereignnations.com/2019/10/11/trojan-horse-ep3-critical-race-theory/.

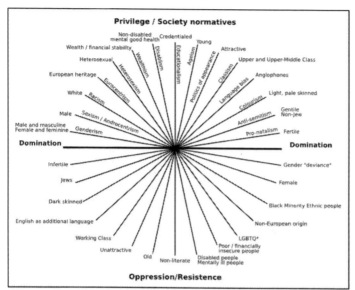

Figure 1. Sheena Erete, Intersecting axes of privilege, domination, and oppression, *ACM Interactions Magazine 25, no. 3, May-June 2018, New York, DOI:10.1145/3194349.*

An essential core belief of these social science theories is power as central to the struggle between the *oppressor* and *oppressed*. Their belief is that society has historically constructed certain numerous hierarchies that violate a particular group of people distinguished by certain characteristics, identifying them by labeled categories, and continually using their abusive power over the weaker in order to subjugate them so as to serve the needs of the stronger. Collins and Bilge put it this way,

> Intersectionality as an analytic tool examines how power relations are intertwined and mutually constructing. Race, class,

gender, sexuality, dis/ability, ethnicity, nation, religion, and age are categories of analysis, terms that reference important social divisions. But they are also categories that gain meaning from power relations of racism, sexism, heterosexism, and class exploitation. One way of describing the organization of power identifies four distinctive yet interconnected domains of power: interpersonal, disciplinary, cultural, and structural.[17]

So, not only is one defined as an oppressor or the oppressed as defined by the sum total of one's personal intersecting categories or characteristics, but also one will hold intrinsic and communal power over others causing them unjust pain and suffering just because of who they are as well. "These systems of injustice are embedded in our society and culture to marginalize, subordinate, and oppress people of color and women. This results in individual and communal suffering."[18]

Conversely, if you are of a lower level you are powerless, disaffected, and victimized and should speak power to those who oppress you. Empowerment, social justice, power, and equity are all catchwords from post-truth centered theories such as critical race theory, with the goal of inverting the assumed, historic, oppressor-oppressed social structure.

According to Intergroup Resources, power is understood within the framework of the critical race and intersectional theories in the following way:

17. Patricia Hill Collins, and Sirma Bilge, *Intersectionality*, 6.
18. Grace Ji-Sun Kim, and Susan M. Shaw, *Intersectional Theology*, Location 939.

Power is unequally distributed globally and in U.S. society; some individuals or groups wield greater power than others, thereby allowing them greater access and control over resources. Wealth, whiteness, citizenship, patriarchy, heterosexism, and education are a few key social mechanisms through which power operates. Although power is often conceptualized as power over other individuals or groups, other variations are power with (used in the context of building collective strength) and power within (which references an individual's internal strength). Learning to "see" and understand relations of power is vital to organizing for progressive social change.[19]

Language Reframing

'When I use a word,' Humpty Dumpty said in rather a scornful tone, 'it means just what I choose it to mean – neither more nor less.' 'The question is,' said Alice, 'whether you can make words mean so many different things.' 'The question is,' said Humpty Dumpty, 'which is to be Master – that's all.'[20] This gives a literary picture of the next tool in the post-truth tool bag called *language reframing*.

Language reframing is changing the language by changing the meanings of words or to create new words with their corresponding definitions. This tactic is to mold a new definition of a word to fit their preconceived and self-made truth narrative and therefore bring conformity to the new meanings and resulting change desired.

19. *White Fragility*, 17, 2019.
20. Lewis Carroll, *Through the Looking Glass*, ePub ed. (Toronto, Ontario, Canada: Harper Perennial Classics, 2015), 63–64.

Unfortunately, these redefined words do not reflect objective reality and meaning. However, if they can say it enough times over a long period of time, then their reward is to hear it as a spoken standard in everyday usage and subsequent behavior.

> This isn't innocent linguistic drift or slang; it is a conscious effort to reshape society. The schemes include redefining words for personal gain, using modifiers to alter the meaning of a word, replacing technical words with colloquial ones, and creating new words. Each of these is a bullying tactic, which distort effective discourse.[21]

One significant example of this subtle shift of redefining of terms (that goes mostly unnoticed by the casual observer) is the word *equality* being replaced by the word *equity*. This is not done by accident, it is intentional. It is part of the retooling of terms in language to fit the narrative of extreme feminism, critical race theory, and intersectionality.

Equity, according to the dictionary, means "the quality of being fair or impartial; fairness; impartiality."[22] By equity, post-truth adherents do not mean the legal and social impartiality between all people regardless of race, gender, or disability. The modern definition of equity means something entirely hidden and subjectively defined.

21. R Benjamin and Dierker, "How The Left's War On Words Manipulates Your Mind," Federalist, May 1, 2018, accessed October 30, 2019, https://thefederalist.com/2018/05/01/lefts-war-words-manipulates-mind/.

22. "Equity," *Lexico*, accessed October 7, 2019, http://www.lexico.com/en/definition/equity.

It is supposed to mean there must be equal outcomes for everyone though its real meaning is Marxian in essence and is not actually for the benefit of everyone. It actually means that some must be rejected under this new order, and a place must be made to put others there regardless if they have earned it or have the qualifications to get there. Psychologist Jordan Peterson, a professor of psychology at the University of Toronto, a clinical psychologist and well-known author, put it this way:

> Equity is a whole different ballgame. It is predicated on the idea that the only certain measure of "equality" is outcome, educational, social, and occupational. The equity-pushers assume axiomatically that if all positions at every level of hierarchy in ever[y] organization are not occupied by a proportion of the population that is precisely equivalent to that proportion in the general population that systemic prejudice (racism, sexism, homophobia, etc.) is definitely at play, and that there are perpetrators who should be limited or punished that have or are currently producing that prejudice.[23]

In other words, instead of sincere equal acknowledgment and respectful treatment of all people regardless of any outward distinguishing traits, those who have been the supposed victims are challenged to turn the tables and now themselves be the ones in

---

23. Jordan Peterson, "Equity: When the Left Goes Too Far," Jordan B. Peterson, accessed October 30, 2019, https://www.jordanbpeterson.com/political-correctness/equity-when-the-left-goes-too-far/.

control *over* their former supposed oppressors. True equality is not the actual goal; getting even is.

The effort to reverse the supposed social position and power of the oppressor over the oppressed through the reshaping of language is evident in many areas of our everyday society and practices. It is another area where better forms of conduct towards those who have suffered various maladies are being used as a segue to social activism.

Post-truth social activism is based on deconstructing and replacing the age-old social constructs of perceived privileged individuals who keep the oppressed in a victimized state and thus have power and control over the weaker and troubled in our society. This arises out of particular theories that purport to clarify reality with their own truth claims and standards so as to change the historic, false hierarchal, and systemic bullying.

One of these theories to advance this equity is called *labeling theory*. In the context of redefining the description of those who are typically called *homeless*, Dr. Geraldine Palmer, managing director of the Community Wellness Institute, portrays it this way:

> In developing the argument that deviance is socially constructed, labeling theorist have borrowed from conflict theory to demonstrate who is labeled, and why. The backdrop of this premise demonstrate[s] that powerful people in society, are the ones who control the labeling process and use it according to their biases and interests. For example, from a critical race perspective, Black/African Americans are more likely than White/European Americans to be labeled criminal or

delinquent, as is people categorized as lower-class versus middle-class. Their actual behavior has no relevance.[24]

The other theory is called *first-person language* and is opposed to the traditional *identity-first language*. "Identity-First Language (IFL) . . . places the disability or disorder first in the description of the person"[25] whereas Person-First Language ostensibly puts their personhood ahead of their labeled condition or status. An example of this is to say with someone with autism is not to be called *autistic* or *autistic person* but rather *a person with autism*. The use of one or the other is continuously debated among practitioners in the area of physical disabilities. Another example is changing the usual reference to someone living on the streets, not as a *homeless person* but rather *a person experiencing homelessness.*[26]

24. Geraldine L. Palmer, "People Who Are Homeless Are "People" First: Opportunity for Community Psychologist to Lead Through Language Reframing," *Global Journal of Community Psychology Practice* 9, no. 2 (November 2018), accessed November 6, 2019, https://www.gjcpp.org/en/article.php?issue=30&article=180.

25. Phillip Ferrigon, "Person-First Language Vs. Identity-First Language: An Examination of the Gains and Drawbacks of Disability Language in Society," *Journal of Teaching Disability Studies* (January 2019), accessed November 6, 2019, https://jtds.commons.gc.cuny.edu/person-first-language-vs-identity-first-language-an-examination-of-the-gains-and-drawbacks-of-disability-language-in-society/.

26. Geraldine L. Palmer, "People Who Are Homeless Are "People" First: Opportunity for Community Psychologist to Lead Through Language Reframing," *Global Journal of Community Psychology Practice* 9, no. 2 (November 2018), accessed November 6, 2019, https://www.gjcpp.org/en/article.php?issue=30&article=180.

The restoring of humanity to a person suffering severe and disabling physical or socio-economic challenges is well-intentioned and noble and should be practiced with anyone and everyone in such situations. Nevertheless, the irony in this approach in trying not to stigmatize people with labels is still essentially re-labeling and categorizing them. The genuine efforts to formulate keener methods of valuing and relating to variously impaired individuals by some are almost imperceptibly commandeered to promote causes for social justice and equity by others. This is evidenced by Dr. Palmer as she discloses the actual motive for such redefining of terms: "...reshaping language can also serve to create spaces where empowerment, wellness and social justice, have room to blossom."[27] The terms of power struggle and justice for groups or categories of persons are the buzzwords of critical race theory and intersectionality. The goal of the renaming is not restoring the humanity of the challenged individual but rather the imposition of a post-truth narrative through the changing of language.

Moreover, the tactic of changing language and the meanings of words has extended beyond the more innocuous areas such as individuals with physical disabilities or in an economic state of homelessness. A glaring example of stretching the person-first language, or labeling theories, into other unrelated areas was recently manifested in San Francisco's criminal justice system. In 2019, San Francisco leaders proposed an entire relabeling of criminals along these lines of reframing language:

27. Palmer, "People Who Are Homeless".

The words "felon," "offender," "convict," "addict" and "juvenile delinquent" would be part of the past in official San Francisco parlance under new "person first" language guidelines adopted by the Board of Supervisors.

Going forward, what was once called a convicted felon or an offender released from jail will be a "formerly incarcerated person," or a "justice-involved" person or simply a "returning resident."

Parolees and people on criminal probation will be referred to as a "person on parole," or "person under supervision."

A juvenile "delinquent" will become a "young person with justice system involvement," or a "young person impacted by the juvenile justice system."

And drug addicts or substance abusers will become "a person with a history of substance use."

"We don't want people to be forever labeled for the worst things that they have done," Supervisor Matt Haney said.

Haney was one of 10 supervisors (Gordon Mar was absent) who voted for the new guidelines, which Supervisor Sandra Lee Fewer proposed.

According to the resolution, 1 of 5 California residents has a criminal record, and words like "prisoner," "convict," "inmate" or "felon" "only serve to obstruct and separate people from society and make the institutionalization of racism and supremacy appear normal," the resolution states.

"Inaccurate information, unfounded assumptions, generalizations and other negative predispositions associated with justice-involved individuals create societal stigmas, attitudinal barriers and continued negative stereotypes," it continues.

"We want them ultimately to become contributing citizens, and referring to them as felons is like a scarlet letter that they can never get away from," Haney said.[28]

Another glaring example of reshaping language is recently seen amongst global warming/climate change activists. The original term climate change was eventually shifted from the term *global warming* to make it more believable and palatable to the public. Now it has been discovered that this term too has lost its luster and losing ground in the minds of people. Their contention is that the world is doomed and within just a few years climate change will cause billions of deaths, leaving us little to almost no time to change things now.

The core problem of this alarmism is that there is no overwhelming and inarguable scientific evidence confirming such a timeclock on worldwide disaster, nor is there agreement among supporting experts in the field as to when this expected extinction will occur. Furthermore, they are promoting the use of alarmist language to frighten people (especially the young) to fit a narrative that is not truly substantiated. Zion Lights, a representative of the climate

28. Phil Matier, "SF Board of Supervisors sanitizes language of criminal justice system," *Local, San Francisco Chronicle*, August 11, 2019, accessed November 6, 2019, https://www.sfchronicle.com/bayarea/philmatier/article/SF-Board-of-Supervisors-sanitizes-language-of-14292255.php?psid=iZG6E.

change organization Extinction Rebellion (known by its acrostic XR), stated as such saying, "alarmist language works."[29]

Aaron Hall of global brand strategy firm Siegel+Gale wrote about the language necessary recently for AdAge: "Is there a better way to convey the urgency of the situation, while also encouraging folks to take action? Could the tools of branding and brand naming create a more resonant, powerful name?"[30] In the same article, he and his team proposed terms to use such as *Scorched Earth* and *Climate Collapse, Climate Chaos* among other proposed terms to arrest public attention and create a sense of urgency (or panic). Hall concludes by saying, "Whatever we call it, impending climate doom is upon us if we don't act quickly. Global leaders have been sluggish, and by and large, individuals have failed to see the need for immediate action. But maybe branding can help. Perhaps a new name will shift the needle, even if just a little."[31]

The altering of the meaning of old terms or the creation of new ones is not a new technique. Reshaping language based on one's own bias and preferences, regardless of objective realities, is a ploy often repeated in recent history. It is indicative of the old quote attributed

29. Thomas D. Williams and Ph.D., "Watch: Extinction Rebellion Spokesperson: 'Alarmist Language Works'," Breitbart, October 10, 2019, accessed December 3, 2019, https://www.breitbart.com/environment/2019/10/10/watch-extinction-rebellion-spokesperson-alarmist-language-works/.

30. Aaron Hall, "Renaming climate change: Can a new name finally make us take action?," AdAge, November 27, 2019, accessed December 3, 2019, http://adage.com/article/industry-insights/renaming-climate-change-can-new-name-finally-make-us-take-action/2218821.

31. Hall, *Renaming Climate Change.*

to Adolf Hitler (or Joseph Goebbels, depending on which source one uses) in which it was said: "If you tell a big enough lie and tell it frequently enough, it will be believed." What makes today's intentional changing of language uniquely post-truth is the forming of a preferred narrative and an influencing of others to not only prefer it as well, but also to believe it through emotional incitement without facts to back it up.

Social Justice

The previously mentioned term social justice is rightly the extension of the intersectional and critical race theory endeavor. It is pervasive in the numerous and critical areas of our culture such as the legal system, politics, media, entertainment, and education. It is the tip of the spear of the current post-truth activism.

What is social justice? According to one source which typifies today's general meaning of the term, "social justice is a structuring of institutions and relationships so that people's basic needs are met, people are treated with equity and fairness, differences are welcomed and valued, and economic, social, political, and religious equality is achieved."[32]

Another source, a textbook on social justice, defines it: "Full and equal participation of all groups in a society that is mutually shaped to meet their needs. Social justice includes a vision of society in which the distribution of resources is equitable and all members of a space,

32. Grace Ji-Sun Kim, and Susan M. Shaw, *Intersectional Theology.*

community, or institution, or society are physically and psychologically safe and secure."[33]

The truth is when you do a search on any Internet search engine, of the over one billion results yielded, you will find no clear definition of social justice. Though there may be some similarities in some of the main themes, a clear, concise, and objective meaning for the term does not actually exist. The difficulty in not having a reliable objective, truth, and evidence-based definition for all to adhere to is that anyone can shape it into what they feel or need it to mean, which is an essential and dangerous post-truth hallmark.

In addition, within the epistemological sphere of social justice, there are numerous subcategories with some variants of definition themselves: health justice, racial justice, economic (distributive) justice, educational justice, procedural justice, restorative justice, and numerous others. The end game for many teachers in our educational system, at all levels, is not to educate but rather to indoctrinate and motivate to provoke social change through their students. Their goal is to get their students to correct the perceived wrongs perpetrated by the oppressors in society and then openly act against it.

This explains the constant problematization, polarization, and activism (sometimes brutally) about almost everything by so many young people at the college and university level. Dr. Jennie Whitcomb, assistant dean for teacher education at the University of Colorado at Boulder, wrote a contributing article in the International

---

33. Maurianne Adams et al., *Teaching for Diversity and Social Justice*, third edition ed. (New York: Routledge, 2016), 1.

Encyclopedia of Education affirming this missional objective with almost evangelistic fervor,

> A social justice approach to teacher education begins with the idea that a central purpose of education is to redress social, economic, and political inequities. Its intellectual roots lie within a radical progressive tradition. In this conception, a good teacher understands socioeconomic and political forces that maintain structural inequality and oppression, including how schools as institutions reinforce the *status quo* and further inequitable educational experiences. Given the centrality of race, ethnicity, and class in inequality, a social justice approach to teaching involves an ongoing commitment to grapple with these matters. A teacher for social justice enacts curriculum so that students develop both a critical social consciousness and the intellectual and practical tools to be agents of change. Students study the experiences of those who have been marginalized along with possibilities for liberation. The teacher also ensures that students learn skills and knowledge associated with the most powerful (cultural capital), thereby helping to promote access to all levels of society. Classrooms are democratic communities where the teacher helps construct an ethos of care and respect. Finally, a social justice teacher also embraces an identity as a community activist and sees this work as an extension of her teaching.[34]

34. J.A. Whitcomb, "Conceptions of Teacher Education," in *International Encyclopedia of Education*, ed. Penelope Peterson, Eva Baker, and Barry McGaw, third edition ed. (Oxford: Elsevier, 2010).

This position, therefore, presents an adversarial role against the home and community instead of an overlapping and supporting role in bringing common and unique knowledge to the youth of our nation. The late Michael Novak, a renowned American Catholic philosopher and journalist who authored over forty books, recognized and warned of this already occurring years ago,

> The trouble with "social justice" begins with the very meaning of the term. Hayek points out that whole books and treatises have been written about social justice without ever offering a definition of it. It is allowed to float in the air as if everyone will recognize an instance of it when it appears. This vagueness seems indispensable. The minute one begins to define social justice, one runs into embarrassing intellectual difficulties. It becomes, most often, a term of art whose operational meaning is, "We need a law against that." In other words, it becomes an instrument of ideological intimidation, for the purpose of gaining the power of legal coercion.[35]

Within Christianity also, the Social Justice movement has taken a deep hold and going deeper and has already threatened the pure message of the Gospel. Though this will be explored more in-depth later, it is sufficient to say here that the current ideal of social justice does not square in the least with the biblical idea of justice. This point is well stated by pastor and writer Dr. Josh Buice,

35. Michael Novak, "Defining Social Justice," *First Things* (December 2000), accessed November 18, 2019,
   http://www.firstthings.com/article/2000/12/defining-social-justice.

Social Justice claims to run to the aid of the oppressed and the victims of discrimination, racism, and other evils of society. What Christian doesn't want to help the oppressed? What Christian wants to turn their back upon the evils of discrimination and racism? The problem with the social justice movement is that it leads to oppression rather than liberation. Social justice fuels the idea of victim status while promoting false ideas of systemic racism and systemic oppression of women within evangelicalism. Finally, social justice often uses political methods and cultural ideas as the answer to these *problems* rather than the sufficient Word of God.[36]

The outstanding problem of incorporating the modern post-truth idea of social justice into the church and the message of the Gospel is that it does not coincide with the actual biblical idea of justice as God defines it, nor does it constitute part of the literal definition of the Gospel or its mission.

The real justice that God establishes is both experiential and eschatological. It is not a part of the actual content and substance of the Gospel message as delineated by Paul clearly in 1 Corinthians 2:2 (NKJV) "For I determined not to know anything among you except Jesus Christ and Him crucified." In 1 Corinthians 15:1-4 Paul defines the Gospel as simply and succinctly as only the message of

36. Josh Buice, "Social Justice is an Attack on the Sufficiency of Scripture,"
    Resources, Statement on Social Justice & the Gospel, September 13, 2018,
    accessed November 18, 2019,
    https://statementonsocialjustice.com/articles/social-justice-is-an-attack-on-the-
    sufficiency-of-Scripture/.

Jesus' death, burial, and resurrection. True justice is a biproduct of the impact of the Gospel now and a significant expression of the future literal kingdom of God on earth.

As concerns the eschatological element of true justice for all people, it is shown in the Scriptures that in God's future literal kingdom on earth that justice will reign supreme:

> Isaiah 11:1-4 (NKJV)—[1] There shall come forth a Rod from the stem of Jesse, and a Branch shall grow out of his roots. [2] The Spirit of the LORD shall rest upon Him, The Spirit of wisdom and understanding, The Spirit of counsel and might, The Spirit of knowledge and of the fear of the LORD. [3] His delight *is* in the fear of the LORD, And He shall not judge by the sight of His eyes, Nor decide by the hearing of His ears; [4] But with righteousness He shall judge the poor, And decide with equity for the meek of the earth; He shall strike the earth with the rod of His mouth, And with the breath of His lips He shall slay the wicked.

The methods of today's social justice movement from within the church are not how God actually brings about justice now or in the future. Pastor Tom Buck of the First Baptist Church of Lindale, Texas correctly clarifies both the practical attitude and the correct biblical understanding that today's church is to have:

> The gospel addresses the root of our problem, which is our need for heart transformation through the gospel of the Lord Jesus Christ. Christ's church is the only institution in this world entrusted with this message. Its mission has never been to fix the

world's social problems. Jesus gave the church "the keys of the kingdom of heaven" not the keys to City Hall.

That is not to say that the bad fruit of injustice around us does not need to be confronted. If we as Christians witness sexual abuse or the evils of racism within the church or denominational structures, we must confront that sin and seek to care for those who are entangled in the web of injustice. Our calling to be faithful gospel ambassadors does not prevent us from confronting sin, in fact, it would demand us to do so.

However, when the Church raises social reform and political methods above the gospel we will find ourselves drifting from our mission. The greatest means by which to change this world is for the church to carry out its God-given task of confronting the root of our problem and offering the only real solution – authentic gospel transformation.

History has exposed the serious danger of the church allowing social reform to interrupt its calling. Churches drifting from the mission of addressing the root of the problem in this world to the fruit of the problem have always led to spiritual disaster. Over time, they began to view the fruit of the problem as the root of the problem and the biblical gospel was replaced with a social gospel – which is no gospel at all (Galatians 1:6-7).

If the church wants to follow the example of Jesus and fulfill its mission, it must use every opportunity to faithfully preach the gospel to all nations. This only happens as the church remains faithful to preach Christ crucified and call all people to repentance and faith in him. Anything else is simply mission drift.[37]

Identity Politics

One of the primary outgrowths of the prominent critical race and intersectionality theories is what is called *identity politics*. What exactly is identity politics? Once again, it is a term popularly used but not unitedly defined. It is a post-truth shaped idea that uses preference and emotion to loosely define something yet remain convincing enough to sway millions to believe it.

> Identity politics are broadly defined, but they typically involve an individual who bases his identity on social categories and divisions. Some examples are a feminist who always votes for female candidates regardless of policies, or a black person who primarily supports causes designed to empower the black community.
>
> The late 20th century saw a rise in identity politics as social injustice and inequality became widely acknowledged. The large political and social movements led to the notion that individuals are more prone to poverty, violence and marginalization based on ethnicity, gender and other social divisions. Identity politics involves embracing these divisions as an essential part of identity,

37. Tom Buck, "The Danger of Mission Drift in the Church," Article, Statement on Social Justice & the Gospel, September 19, 2018, accessed December 7, 2019, https://statementonsocialjustice.com/articles/the-danger-of-mission-drift-in-the-church/.

which means the identity of a single person is necessarily politicized by the social categories to which he belongs.[38]

The concept is to classify people according to their groups, according to how they identify themselves based on mutual attributes such as race, gender, political party, certain values or beliefs similarly held, or any other countless number of attributes of similarity. When these groups are organized and motivated, they then pursue a change in society to defend, promote, or protect their group identity through the tool of politics. Jonathan Rauch, Senior Fellow at the Brookings Institution and a contributing editor at *The Atlantic*, attempts a definition of identity politics: "Identity politics" is a hard term to pin down, but a reasonable working definition would be: political mobilization organized around group characteristics such as race, gender, and sexuality, as opposed to party, ideology, or pecuniary interest."[39]

Authors Greg Lukianoff and Jonathan Haidt describe identity politics as consisting of two types: *common-humanity identity politics* and *common-enemy identity politics*. With common-humanity identity politics he relates how Dr. Martin Luther King, Jr., and others used this approach: "Instead of shaming or demonizing their opponents, they humanized them and then relentlessly appealed to their

---

38. "What Are Examples of Identity Politics?," Types of Government, Reference, accessed November 25, 2019, https://www.reference.com/government-politics/examples-identity-politics-93ea56a0dfa41095.

39. Jonathan Rauch, "Speaking as A...," *The New York Review of Books* 64, no. 17 (November 2017).

humanity."[40] The second type, common-enemy identity politics, is "based on an effort to unite and mobilize multiple groups to fight against a common enemy."[41] The post-truth world of today uses the common-enemy form of identity politics without discretion, and it is this form that is utilized by the media in all its forms, by politicians, and mainly by self-styled social justice groups and activists with neo-Marxian roots.

Though a familiar historic technique in politics worldwide, this common-enemy form of identity politics has a major adverse effect on the culture by categorizing and grouping people at the loss of the individual's identity. The other degrading effect it has on the people is explained by Mike Gonzalez of the Heritage Foundation:

> It instead looks at America through a post–modernist lens of power struggles among groups based on race, ethnicity or sex, but where the individual loses agency. It resegregates America into subnational "protected" groupings whose members receive benefits simply as a consequence of group membership and in whose name self-appointed leaders demand unequal treatment.[42]

40. Greg Lukianoff and Jonathan Haidt, *The Coddling of the American Mind: How Good Intentions and Bad Ideas Are Setting up a Generation for Failure* (New York City: Penguin Books, 2019), 61.

41. Lukianoff and Haidt, *The Coddling Of*, 61.

42. Mike Gonzalez, "It Is Time to Debate – and End – Identity Politics" Commentary, The Heritage Foundation, October 9, 2018, accessed December 8, 2019 https://www.heritage.org/civil-society/commentary/it-time-debate-and-end-identity-politics.

In Revelation 5:9-10 (NKJV) we see the result of the true Gospel which denies identity politics by default because it unites all people of all ethnic origins and skin color into one body equally and beautifully under King Jesus through His unadulterated Gospel: "[9] And they sang a new song, saying: "You are worthy to take the scroll, And to open its seals; For You were slain, And have redeemed us to God by Your blood Out of every tribe and tongue and people and nation, [10] And have made us kings and priests to our God; And we shall reign on the earth."

Dr. Albert Mohler, president of the Southern Baptist Theological Seminary, accurately lays out the clearest biblical position concerning post-truth identity politics and it is necessarily included here in its entirety:

> The biblical worldview is the only antidote to identity politics. Intersectionality erodes the bedrock of civil society and dismantles decorum precisely because it is predicated and upon differences. It will only tolerate and celebrate divergence and divisiveness. The Christian worldview, however, offers a powerful response to identity politics. The biblical reply does not deny the reality nor the importance of identities to the human story. It does, however, begin with what unites all humanity— the Imago Dei. The biblical worldview starts in sameness not differences. It grounds the value of an individual in something more transcendent than experience, background, race, or gender; it starts with the image of God that resides in every human being on the planet. Humanity stands united by virtue of our common descent from Adam and Eve. Christians, therefore, do not reject

identity politics and intersectionality merely because of its failure as an ideology, but because it denies the common bond that beats in the heart of every human: we are all made in God's image. That identity is precious, perennial, and most to be cherished.

By the way, this issue helps to underline why biblically committed Christians must point again and again to the common descent of all humanity from Adam and Eve. We all share the same first parents. Modern evolutionary theory denies the very possibility of common descent from a single couple. Ideas have consequences.

Christians must understand and hold fast to the image of God that unites humanity in a common identity. The most important identity for every human is not our own self-prescribed definition based upon their experiences and background, but the identity given to them by the God of the universe. That identity trumps everything else.

Additionally, the biblical argument is not drawn only from Genesis. It reaches not only into the truths of Genesis, but the glories of the New Covenant of redemption inaugurated by Christ. Jesus Christ is creating a new humanity—a people not of this world but of heaven, a people for God's pleasure. It is a people made up of every tribe, tongue, people, and language—a citizenry of every ethnicity and race, of every socio-economic background and culture. Its citizenship does not stand on its differences but on our common salvation in Christ. In Christ we find our true identity. Believers in Christ share an eternal and glorious unity in Jesus Christ the Lord—a unity we enter upon faith in Jesus's perfect sacrifice and atonement for sin

Intersectionality and identity politics breed division. These ideologies atomize society and drive humanity away from its core and essential commonality. This is where Christians must counter with the gospel of Jesus Christ and the authority of Scripture. Only the gospel secures peace and establishes truth. Only the gospel will unite a fractured society. Only the gospel can stem the tide of modernity's downward spiral into chaos and decay. Identity politics is bad enough in the culture. In the church, it denies the gospel altogether.

Of this, I am certain: At the marriage supper of the Lamb, no one will hold any kind of sign claiming their own identity.[43]

---

43. Albert Mohler, "The Power of the Gospel and the Meltdown of Identity Politics," Article, Albert Mohler, February 12, 2019, accessed December 7, 2019, http://albertmohler.com/2019/02/12/power-gospel-meltdown-identity-politics.

Chapter 11

Post-truth as a Religion

Belief systems that are post-truth (and often coupled with postmodernism) have often been described as becoming a religion in and of themselves. This is due to the alignment of its attributes with the typical characteristics of a religion. These characteristics basically exhibit themselves as having a common guidebook, a common creed based on a set of cardinal beliefs, a born-again experience or conversion, a lifestyle of purity, a system of discipline of errant members, a utopian vision of how it will be one day, an evangelistic mission to bring others into the fold with a method of training.

It can be argued that the most prominent post-truth notions that are religious-like and hegemonic in our society are Intersectionality and critical race theory. The characteristics of their paradigms parallel those of religion in the following way:

- The original sin for which all white people, in particular, are helplessly born into is racism or oppression, especially if a white person is a white male. This state of sinfulness is unavoidable and the cost of converting away from it is decisive and costly.

- To be redeemed from this sin, post-truth ideologies provide no human or human-like god or messiah-savior (i.e., Jesus for Christianity). However, there is a type of salvation (i.e., the proverbial "come-to-Jesus moment") which is called being woke.

- The parallel of living in purity is maintaining one's wokeness (e.g., awareness) concerning racial and social issues that arise daily.

- For those who have followed this religion of wokeness but then deviate from the beliefs or methods, there is a form of discipline by the congregation and its leaders. They can be thrown out or excommunicated if they open their mind to discuss contrary ideas with others of other belief systems, show the beginnings of doubt, or refuse to go all-in with the ideas of these race theories.

- There is to be a complete separation from the world that opposes or questions their beliefs and ideals.

- The utopian goal they wish to reach is a world without the systemic hate and previous centuries-long subjugation of certain groups of people by other more dominant ones.

- To usher in this age one day, we are all to be evangelistic in community activism, permeate the institutions that form and shape the culture, and bring others into the cause, and then training them to believe more purely and do the same with others.

- Their holy texts are the writings and speeches of those who author and lead organizations that preach the gospel of equity and justice.

For example, American attorney, journalist, and author David French observed the religious-like movement that is intersectionality in this way:

"For the in group, it's easy to see the appeal of the philosophy. There's an animating purpose -- fighting injustice, racism and inequality. There's the original sin of "privilege." There's a conversion experience -- becoming "woke." And much as the Christian church puts a premium on each person's finding his or her precise role in the body of Christ, intersectionality can provide a person with a specific purpose and role based on individual identity and experience."[1]

Today, due to the decades of postmodern doubt of the existence of absolute truth, and with today's post-truth rejection of self-evident absolute truths, a vacuum in the minds and hearts of people has been created and is ever widening. The oft-quoted statement attributed to Aristotle states that nature abhors a vacuum. Christianity echoes this idea illustratively that due to our sinfulness, each of us has a God-shaped vacuum within our soul that only God can fill.

The apostle Paul, under inspiration of God the Holy Spirit, discusses the reason for this God-shaped vacuum in Romans 1:18-25,

> For the wrath of God is revealed from heaven against all ungodliness and unrighteousness of men, who suppress the truth in unrighteousness, because what may be known of God is manifest in them, for God has shown it to them. For since the creation of the world His invisible attributes are clearly seen, being understood by the things that are made, even His eternal power and Godhead, so that they are without excuse, because, although they knew God, they did not glorify Him as God, nor were thankful, but became futile in their thoughts, and their foolish hearts were darkened. Professing to be wise, they became fools, and changed the glory of the incorruptible God into an

1. David French, "Intersectionality is our new national religion," Opinion, Dallas Morning News, March 9, 2018, accessed December 5, 2019, https://www.dallasnews.com/opinion/commentary/2018/03/09/intersectionality-is-our-new-national-religion/.

image made like corruptible man—and birds and four-footed animals and creeping things. Therefore God also gave them up to uncleanness, in the lusts of their hearts, to dishonor their bodies among themselves, who exchanged the truth of God for the lie, and worshiped and served the creature rather than the Creator, who is blessed forever. Amen.

This section of Scripture establishes a fundamental reality of our world. By default, in Adam, man only knew, enjoyed, and worshiped God the Creator. Through man's sin and rebellion, an emptiness has since existed in every person's heart, soul and mind which creates a need to fill it in other ways that bring a sense of belonging and purpose for living.

Since the sin of Adam and Eve, mankind's ordinary worship of God has been rejected, suppressed and replaced by worship of the creature rather than the Creator, exalting even himself above God (Gen. 11:1-9). By this, we understand that if God is considered non-existent to mankind, then he will find another god to fill that void regardless. As the rock singer Bob Dylan said in one of his famous songs, "you're gonna have to serve somebody."[2]

Today, people are lost and have an erroneous, vain understanding of the real world and of the solutions truly needed to provide fulfillment and peace for the individual and the culture as a whole. The world system that is driven by Satan through man's vain thinking is skillfully fed by influential and powerful disseminators of

2. Bob Dylan, "Ya Gotta Serve Somebody," in *Slow Train Coming* (New York: Columbia, 1979).

untruth, propounding man-centered belief systems and solutions. These then take on the identity of a self-made religion to which they zealously dedicate their time, energy, effort, and finances.

These religious-like belief systems that fill the deeper void within have arisen currently in the form of intersectionality and critical race theories (among other tangential concepts), including a resurfacing of socialism and Marxism. David French continues by saying, "The demise of religion among American youth is greatly exaggerated. It turns out that America isn't raising a new generation of unbelievers. Instead, rising in the heart of deep-blue America are the zealots of a new religious faith. They're the intersectionals. They're fully woke, and the heretics don't stand a chance."[3]

This blind acceptance of the prevailing post-truth groupthink of today is part of what is also testified to in the Scriptures. One of the key passages that describes this vividly and prophetically is found in 2 Thessalonians 2:11-12, "And for this reason God will send them strong delusion, that they should believe the lie, that they all may be condemned who did not believe the truth but had pleasure in unrighteousness."

With postmodernism's deconstruction of Judeo-Christian based values, a hole has been created that is being filled by the advancing religion of post-truth belief systems. This shift into a post-truth society will necessarily make America and the West into a *post-Christian* society.[4] "A Post-Truth society is the only logical end of a

3. French, *Intersectionality Is Our New.*

4. Dickerson, *Hope of Nations*, 31. "That a society is post-Christian does not mean
   the nation has no Christians; it means the society has abandoned Christianity as

post-Christian society. Post-Truth is the only possible next step for a culture that once founded itself on Christian truths and ideals but now abhors Christian truth to the extent that it will deny Christianity's role in its history."[5] A post-Christian culture and a post-truth one inexorably go hand-in-hand.

its stabilizing center. Christian values are no longer a driving influence in shaping the culture."

5. Dickerson, *Hope of Nations*, 23.

Chapter 12

Post-truth Influence in Christianity

Post-truth affects all areas of an individual's life, which includes that which is extremely important to many if not most people – the area of faith, and in particular, the only true faith: biblical Christianity.

Of the most particular concern in this book is the subversion of the Gospel by post-truth thinking and belief. Interestingly enough, the post-truth denial and replacing of objective truth is fast infiltrating the one faith that historically holds to foundational, objective, and immutable truths and beliefs.

Wittingly and unwittingly, there are many Christians who have accepted these post-truth-based philosophies, thus explaining the weakening of the church before the world. This acceptance by some believers in biblically based churches is not surprising as it is not the first time worldly and heretical ideas have infiltrated the church and carried away many who follow them. Murray addresses this:

> A common phrase in Christian circles is that the church is supposed to be "in but not of" the broader culture. In other words, Christians are to engage with the culture but not be unduly influenced by it. But so pervasive and seductive is the post-truth mindset that the church, at least to some degree, has become in and of the Culture of Confusion.[1]

Paul the apostle warned of this in 2 Timothy 4:3 (NKJV), "For the time will come when they will not endure sound doctrine, but according to their own desires, because they have itching ears, they will heap up for themselves teachers;"

In the culture and behavior of the church, there are two areas in which post-truth has made some insidious inroads. The first is that of how we approach the secular world and manage our standing privately and publicly before unbelievers.

One of the major values propounded universally by the post-truth throngs is *tolerance*. Yet a major conflict arises because post-truth tolerance of today does not match up with the historic and traditional meaning of the word. It becomes an issue of two people saying the same word but meaning two different things. Christian apologists Josh and Sean McDowell define historic tolerance in this way: "Traditional tolerance values, respects, and accepts the

1. Murray, *Saving Truth*, 29.

individual without necessarily approving of or participating in that person's beliefs or behavior."[2]

The post-truth tolerance which dominates today at all levels of society involves not only the acceptance of the other individual in a humane, kind, and respectful manner but also accepting their beliefs and behavior as equally valid and authoritative regardless of their position. The McDowells clarify the difficulty in meanings:

> "This new tolerance, what we will call cultural tolerance, propagates the notion that there is no hierarchy of moral truth—all truth is equal. In traditional tolerance you grant another the right to believe and behave differently without agreeing that he or she is right. Not so with cultural tolerance. What has shifted is the equality of beliefs, values, and truth claims. In other words, not only do all people have a right to believe what they want, but no one's beliefs, values, or truth claims are any more valid than another person's. Essentially, cultural tolerance means all truth is subjective, and thus no individual truth claim should be judged or condemned as wrong.[3]

This is a problem both generationally and culturally. The one person expresses their beliefs and obedience to the absolute truths God has established, and the other person believes and shows the new post-truth idea of tolerance.

2. Josh McDowell and Sean McDowell, *The Beauty of Intolerance: Setting a Generation Free to Know Truth & Love* (Uhrichsville, Ohio: Shiloh Run Press, an imprint of Barbour Publishing,, 2016), 40.
3. McDowell and McDowell, *The Beauty of Intolerance*, 41.

Additionally, the danger of today's believers and many of their churches is the temptation to soften or weaken not only their approach, but also their understanding and acceptance of what the Bible teaches. The lightning rod of all issues over which now many Christians disagree is the acceptance of homosexuality and same-sex marriage.

In a recent article in the Washington Post, it shows a change in evangelical Protestants concerning this issue: "Even among the most resistant religious group, white evangelical Protestants like the Augustine family, support for same-sex marriage has grown from 11 percent in 2004 to 29 percent in 2019, according to Pew."[4]

This reflects the drift among Christians to water down the Gospel and God's truth. This drift is the result of poorly trained Bible teachers and shifting positions to fit the most recent trends in belief. Other factors creating this drift are the simple desire to avoid conflict with family or friends, or to avert being dismissed from their teaching position. Abdu Murray aptly summarizes the intent and consequence of such wavering by followers of Jesus by saying, "The post-truth Culture of Confusion elevates preferences and feelings over facts and truth. And by elevating our preferences to be liked and feel accepted,

4. Samantha Schmidt, "Americans' views flipped on gay rights. How did minds change so quickly?," Social Issues, Washington Post, June 7, 2019, accessed December 5, 2019, https://www.washingtonpost.com/local/social-issues/americans-views-flipped-on-gay-rights-how-did-minds-change-so-quickly/2019/06/07/ae256016-8720-11e9-98c1-e945ae5db8fb_story.html.

Christians have misapplied the plain truth of Jesus' words and exchanged them for pleasant cultural comforts."[5]

The most dangerous reason for such a shift that affects the content and effective sharing of the Gospel itself is the wholesale acceptance of the world's post-truth beliefs and inserting them into the Bible, manipulating what it clearly says to the contrary. In either case, the compromise is at alarming levels, already, and continues to grow.

Abdu Murray speaks to this dissonance:

> Let's address the first post-truth seduction: making the gospel pill easier to swallow to avoid uncomfortable discussions with non-Christians and difficult Bible passages that challenge our behavioral preferences. In our effort to be liked, Jesus' famous statement, "Judge not lest ye be judged," is often misquoted. Many, including those in the church, interpret this passage to mean that Jesus shunned moral judgment. And, so the argument goes, Christians have no place judging the actions of others in the broader culture.[6]

The most prominent post-truth belief that not only dominates in our culture today but also infiltrates the American church is intersectionality and critical race theory. It is affecting both theology and the content and message of the Gospel itself. Theology is to be based on the literal-grammatical-historical method of interpreting the Bible and based on that it is systematized for an organized

5. Murray, *Saving Truth*, 33.
6. Murray, *Saving Truth*, 31.

understanding of the many great truths of God revealed in His Word. It is based on exegesis of the Word of God, not eisegesis. "Exegesis and eisegesis are two conflicting approaches in Bible study. Exegesis is the exposition or explanation of a text based on a careful, objective analysis. The word *exegesis* literally means 'to lead out of.' That means that the interpreter is led to his conclusions by following the text."[7] In short, exegesis reads from the text, eisegesis reads into the text.

It is therefore alarming how post-truth ideals are being increasingly read into previously sound theology in order to shape it into how one wants God to be, not according to the God that is. Theologians and professors Grace Ji-Sun Kim and Susan M. Shaw, in their book *Intersectional Theology: An Introductory Guide,* unashamedly endorse and promote such an approach:

> Traditionally, theology has assumed a white, male, heterosexual, able-bodied subject with very little self reflection on the impact of theologians' social location on theology. In other words, for most of Christian history, straight white male theologians have spoken for everyone else, as if their theologies do not reflect the bias of their own social positions and power. This has meant that our theologies have been partial, a reflection of only a very small slice of the whole of human experience. In many ways, we have missed out on a great deal we could have learned about God and ourselves by ignoring and subordinating the experiences and theological reflections of most of humanity. An intersectional center demands that theology attend to difference and power and

---

7. "What is the difference between exegesis and eisegesis?," Got Questions, accessed December 26, 2019, http://www.gotquestions.org/exegesis-eisegesis.html.

recognize the significant contributions to theology from diverse contributors and the limitations of theologies that only reflect a dominant or single-axis view.[8]

Another subtle but substantial example from the theologically conservative side of Christianity demonstrates again how powerful this has become and how deeply it has taken root. In one of the Southern Baptist Convention's 2019 resolutions, it states[9] "On Critical Race Theory And Intersectionality" it states: "RESOLVED, That critical race theory and intersectionality should only be employed as analytical tools subordinate to Scripture—not as transcendent ideological frameworks;…"[10]

In this one of twenty-nine statements within the resolution, this one line is dubbed by atheist and mathematics scholar James Lindsay as "a very fine wooden horse sitting outside your gates" or the

8. Grace Ji-Sun Kim, and Susan M. Shaw, *Intersectional Theology*, Location 264-265.
9. "Resolutions," Resolutions Search, Southern Baptist Convention, accessed December 6, 2019, http://www.sbc.net/resolutions/search/. A resolution has traditionally been defined as an expression of opinion or concern, as compared to a motion, which calls for action. A resolution is not used to direct an entity of the Southern Baptist Convention to specific action other than to communicate the opinion or concern expressed. Resolutions are passed during the annual Convention meeting.
10. "On Critical race theory And Intersectionality," Birmingham, AL - 2019, Southern Baptist Convention, 2019, accessed December 6, 2019, http://www.sbc.net/resolutions/2308/resolution-9--on-critical-race-theory-and-intersectionality.

proverbial Trojan Horse. [11] Dr. Lindsay (mentioned before in another context) is also an atheist who makes his observation and warning even more remarkable. In every area where these two secular theories are introduced, they create a conundrum that eventually will make the original foundational tenets of biblical Christian theology almost unrecognizable.

One of the staunch defenders of the faith within the Southern Baptist Convention, Dr. Albert Mohler, in his personal podcast on June 14, appropriately and vehemently criticized the above-mentioned resolution by saying,

> Ideas, as we know, do have consequences, and one of the most lamentable consequences, but the main consequence of critical race theory and intersectionality is identity politics, and identity politics can only rightly be described, as antithetical to the gospel of Jesus Christ. We have to see identity politics as disastrous for the culture and nothing less than devastating for the church of the Lord Jesus Christ. [12]

11. "Trojan Horse (n.)," *The Merriam-Webster.com Dictionary*, https://www.merriam-webster.com/dictionary/Trojan%20horse. After besieging the walls of Troy for ten years, the Greeks built a huge, hollow wooden horse, secretly filled it with armed warriors, and presented it to the Trojans as a gift for the goddess Athena, and the Trojans took the horse inside the city's walls. That night, the armed Greeks swarmed out and captured and burned the city. A Trojan horse is thus anything that looks innocent but, once accepted, has power to harm or destroy—for example, a computer program that seems helpful but ends up corrupting or demolishing the computer's software.

12. Albert Mohler, "Part III Ideas Have Consequences: Critical race theory and Intersectionality in the News from the Southern Baptist Convention," *The*

Disturbingly, it was revealed soon after that a professor of the very same seminary over which Mohler presides, responded in an interview earlier the same year, that he has been positively influenced by the post-truth theories of intersectionality and critical race theory:

Q: What books have most shaped your understanding of racial justice?

A: So many. A few are: Michael Emerson's Divided by Faith; Christena Cleveland's Disunity in Christ; Richard Delgado's Critical race theory: An Introduction; Benjamin Isaac's The Invention of Racism in Classical Antiquity; Love L. Sechrest's A Former Jew: Paul and the Dialectics of Race; and W. E. B. Dubois's The Souls of Black Folks."

Q: Which book do you wish every evangelical Christian would read and why?

A: Richard Delgado's Critical race theory: An Introduction. A necessary book because evangelicals still tend to be decades behind on critical race discussions.

Michael Emerson's Divided by Faith. This book shows how evangelical movement and white supremacy are closely connected. Evangelicals tend to ignore racial discussions because evangelicalism has historically benefited from racism. This book will help evangelicals see this and hopefully move them to repent.

Briefing (June 2019), accessed December 13, 2019,
https://albertmohler.com/2019/06/14/briefing-6-14-19.

Kevin Jones and Jarvis J. Williams's Removing the Stain of Racism from the SBC: Diverse African American and White Perspectives. This book offers a critique of and some solutions to racism in the SBC, the world's largest Protestant evangelical denomination.[13]

These are parasitic and infectious ideals that create division in the church and destroy the content and mission of the Gospel. It is one thing to be accurately informed of a philosophy, and it is another thing to make it a tool to go alongside divinely given absolute truths. To give intersectionality and critical race theory (and any other worldly philosophies), a place of legitimacy within biblical thinking and behavior is asking for division, confusion, and eventual destruction of the substance and mission of the Gospel of Jesus Christ.

A stark example of this kind of corruption of sound theology and its practice in daily life occurred in reaction to a highly emotional scene in a courtroom in Dallas, Texas, in late 2019. The defendant, a white female police officer, saw a black man in what she had mistaken as her apartment which was a floor below. Stating she believed it was an intruder, she shot and killed him. She was found guilty of murder and sentenced to 10 years in prison. What transpired

---

13. Matt Smethurst, "On My Shelf: Life and Books with Jarvis Williams," U.S. Edition, Gospel Coalition, February 28, 2017, accessed December 13, 2019, https://www.thegospelcoalition.org/article/on-my-shelf-life-and-books-with-jarvis-williams/. Interview of Dr. Jarvis Williams, Associate Professor of New Testament Interpretation, Southern Baptist Theological Seminary.

immediately after the sentencing by the jury and the judge was stunning and unforgettable as described in this article:

> Jean's brother, Brandt Jean, addressed the former officer directly from the witness stand, saying that his brother would have wanted her to turn her life over to Christ, and that if she asks God for forgiveness, she will get it.
>
> "I love you as a person. I don't wish anything bad on you," he said before asking the judge, "I don't know if this is possible, but can I give her a hug?"
>
> The judge said OK, and Brandt and Guyger stood up, met in front of the bench and embraced while Guyger cried.
>
> The judge also came down off the bench and hugged a sobbing Guyger before she was led from the courtroom. In addition, the judge opened a Bible to a certain passage and gave it to her. A black bailiff in the courtroom patted the defendant's hair.[14]

Further details from other sources revealed the judge gave the condemned individual her own personal Bible then pointed out John 3:16 to her, instructing her to read it, the Gospels, and the book of John in particular. The biblical and Christ-centered response displayed in that courtroom was a visible display of racial reconciliation, forgiveness, and the untainted Gospel.

14. Jake Bleiberg, "Ex-Dallas cop in deadly shooting gets hug from the judge," Star Tribune, October 3, 2019, accessed December 5, 2019, http://www.startribune.com/slain-man-s-brother-judge-hug-ex-cop-sentenced-to-10-years/562039002/.

It was predictable to hear the secular reactions bemoaning such a religious action done by a public authority in a public courtroom. What is disconcerting are the adverse reactions of some evangelicals to this open display of repentance and reconciliation. It reveals how deeply post-truth has sunk into the conscience of professed believers, as seen in this article in Christianity Today:

> As Americans Christians, we often long for snapshots that make us feel good. We want anecdotes of grace. But in the hurry to resolve painful and uncomfortable stories, we rush past the systemic injustice that lies beneath. Even in the face of overwhelming evidence of racism in our criminal justice system, too many of us remain stoically convinced that injustice is only personal, and rarely, if ever, systemic.
>
> When a black person extends radical forgiveness, we see the grace of the gospel. But when we ignore a black person's call for justice, we cheapen that grace. Both are acting like the God we serve; we need to listen to them both.
>
> Yes, God is a forgiving God. But we haven't really understood the depth of that grace if all our examples of forgiveness are times when the people being forgiven look just like us. Given the long history of white supremacy in this country, we as Christians should ask: Why aren't there videos of white people forgiving their black assailants trending on our social media? Why aren't black accusers hugged by judges or

comforted by the victim's family members, as this former police officer was? How long O Lord?[15]

What the author of this article profoundly forgets is that forgiveness and reconciliation *are* the justice. The buzzwords in this article - systemic injustice, white supremacy, white people - expose the actual thinking and motivation behind it. It does not reveal a careful biblically based response. What it reveals is an entrenchment of post-truth creeds in their mind and hearts that eclipse the doctrinal foundation and attitude of love, mercy, and grace of the true Gospel. The author of this article and those like her, as all followers of Christ, would do well to reflect the attitude as commanded by Jesus in Matthew 5:43-4 (NKJV):

> [43] "You have heard that it was said, 'You shall love your neighbor and hate your enemy.' [44] But I say to you, love your enemies, bless those who curse you, do good to those who hate you, and pray for those who spitefully use you and persecute you, [45] that you may be sons of your Father in heaven; for He makes His sun rise on the evil and on the good, and sends rain on the just and on the unjust. [46] For if you love those who love you, what reward have you? Do not even the tax collectors do the same? [47] And if you greet your brethren only, what do you do more than others?

15. Dorena Williamson, "Botham Jean's Brother's Offer of Forgiveness Went Viral. His Mother's Calls for Justice Should Too.," Speaking Out, Christianity Today, October 4, 2019, accessed December 5, 2019, http://www.christianitytoday.com/ct/2019/october-web-only/botham-jean-forgiveness-amber-guyger.html.

Do not even the tax collectors do so? [48] Therefore you shall be perfect, just as your Father in heaven is perfect.

Chapter 13

The Gospel and Post-truth Fallacies

We have already analyzed and presented critiques of some of the post-truth beliefs in our world. Now we will expose the most blatant fallacies of core post-truth principles and bring a definitive biblical response to each of them.

Feelings Based Belief Versus Truth Based Belief

To understand post-truth thinking, it is best to grasp the context and background of absolute truth-based thinking first. The contrast between the truth-based mind and a post-truth mind is that each defaults to opposing and unreconcilable reference points, respectively. John Dickerson clarifies this fundamental contrast in his book *Hope of Nations*: "Truth-Based thinkers look to an outside, fixed, unchanging written standard to define right and wrong. Post-Truth thinkers look only to their feelings, intuitions, cultural norms, and others to define right and wrong."[1]

An objective-based truth thinker (whether a person of faith or not) turns to the traditions of the Judeo-Christian ethic that are ultimately based on principles in the Word of God. This ethic is based on an originalist interpretation, or rather, an objective, grammatical-historical-literal hermeneutic of the Bible. Similarly, in matters of daily life and practice as a citizen of the United States of America, the truth-based thinker (Christian or not) relies on the Constitution (based on an originalist interpretation) as the objective standard in a similar manner.

These documents have been the prime authoritative source for many years in the United States, even though its establishment and efficacy are being challenged more seriously every day by both postmodern and post-truth forces. Post-truth is a rejection, or a rebellion, against divinely established, tested, and ennobled laws which have lasted for centuries and still stand as such today. Postmodernism decries objective standards as constructs by local human hierarchies and is unknowable, which therefore makes them invalid. Post-truth ignores objective truth and disengages from it entirely, creating its own truth based on the opinions and feelings of the day.

1. Dickerson, *Hope of Nations*, 84.

Because the post-truth thinker relies upon feelings and opinions, they are not guided by nor conform to such transcendent writings, especially in the case of older writings. Dickerson comments on this, "In the simplest sense, a Post-Truth ideology is a view of the world in which reality and morality are defined by a person's emotions, feelings, local culture, or subjective personal criteria rather than by objective facts or fixed standards, such as written law or immutable principles."[2] To identify and understand the post-truth thinker of today, these are several of their most recognizable attributes as enumerated by Dickerson :

> (1) hesitant to critique any outside culture, religion, or way of life, (2) repulsed by traditional American claims of morality or absolute truth, (3) eager to promote exotic ideologies without examining the impact on human rights, (4) prejudiced against any truth claim that originates in the Christianized West, including the Bible, Judeo-Christian ethics, Christian morals, or patriotism, (5) conditioned to be suspicious of or even prejudiced against certain classes that they've been trained to view as oppressors (for example, rich white males, Christians, etc.).[3]

Dickerson likewise outlines the general characteristics of truth-based thinkers:

> (1) They hold objective standards of truth to be more authoritative than personal experience. Pervasively, those standards in the US have been the Bible, Christian values, and

2. Dickerson, *Hope of Nations*, 84.
3. Dickerson, *Hope of Nations*, 95.

the US Constitution, (2) they are eager to critique, and weigh truth claims because they have been taught to pursue the truth, (3) they can disagree with a person about "the truth" without hating the person—because truth is a separate party from the disagreement. Truth is a third party, (4) they value factual accuracy. (5) they can be condescending or closed-minded toward ideologies they deem to be false. (6) they can lack grace when defending the truth.[4]

It is noteworthy in the previous quotation that some criticisms of truth-based thinkers are mentioned. This reflects the intellectual honesty of truth-based thinking. The truth is not just in facts and objective standards, but in how they are applied without prejudice to all people. In post-truth thinking, this kind of humility and honest self-reflection is neither normal nor observed very often.

Since the post-truth mindset is steered by flawed feelings and logic, it then can only draw from the predominant public values and rules of the current period. Additionally, the central core value of society today when deciding what is right or wrong is if the action will hurt anyone. When one's feelings have been hurt by the spoken beliefs or decisions of another in absolute terms, the expected response is that he is *offended*. Abdu Murray notes this observation as well: "In a post-truth age, if the evidence fits our preferences and opinions, then all is well and good. If it doesn't, then the evidence is deemed inadmissible or offensive, with the offense being a kind of solvent against otherwise sound arguments."[5]

4. Dickerson, *Hope of Nations*, 102.
5. Murray, *Saving Truth*, 14.

The overriding value of not offending someone is undergirded by the unspoken rule of never questioning another person's choices, opinions, or judgments. Dickerson shares an example of an extension of this post-truth code of conduct: "And so, for a Post-Truth thinker, it is immoral and condescending to tell people from other cultures that their morality or behavior is wrong."[6] If it hurts another person's feelings, then whatever the truth-based thinker proposes is automatically invalidated and discarded because he is considered closed-minded and absolutist. Furthermore, the demeanor of the post-truth thinker is reactionary, believing that if you disagree with someone's views, then you disrespect or hate them.

It is not surprising then that many Christians are continually being condemned for hating others because they disagree with their beliefs or lifestyle choices that are contrary to the plain reading and meaning of the Bible. What is surprising, and tragic, is that a growing number of professing Christians today also accuse other believers of disrespect and hatred of those who believe and live contrary to biblical teaching, even if those believers are demonstrating a loving and respectful comportment in expressing their disagreement.

The fallout from this type of feelings-based thinking is that those in the post-truth age stop using independent cogent thought and reasoning. As American social theorist and economist Thomas Sowell said, "The problem isn't that Johnny can't read. The problem

6. Dickerson, *Hope of Nations*, 85.

isn't even that Johnny can't think. The problem is that Johnny doesn't know what thinking is; he confuses it with feeling."[7]

For more than a generation, most educators have not been training young people how to think critically and rationally for themselves but instead are propagandizing them with biased information. In addition, rational analysis is passed over for only presumed experts to do for others. This leaves the average person utterly vulnerable to a wholesale acceptance of postmodern and post-truth doctrines without rebuttal. Allen Bloom, in his classic book *The Closing of the American Mind*, lays this out by what he was seeing thirty-two years ago:

> The danger they have been taught to fear from absolutism is not error but intolerance. Relativism is necessary to openness; and this is the virtue, the only virtue, which all primary education for more than fifty years has dedicated itself to inculcating. Openness—and the relativism that makes it the only plausible stance in the face of various claims to truth and various ways of life and kinds of human beings—is the great insight of our times. The true believer is the real danger. The study of history and of culture teaches that all the world was mad in the past; men always thought they were right, and that led to wars, persecutions, slavery, xenophobia, racism, and chauvinism. The point is not to correct the mistakes and really be right; rather it is not to think you are right at all.[8]

7. Potter and Estren, *Question Authority to Think*, 1121.
8. Allan Bloom, *The Closing of the American Mind* (New York, N.Y: Simon and Schuster, 1987), 29.

The attitude of the post-truth thinker feels that to disagree or criticize another's views is to be bigoted and condescending. Bloom also experienced and observed this years ago:

> So indiscriminateness is a moral imperative because its opposite is discrimination. This folly means that men are not permitted to seek for the natural human good and admire it when found, for such discovery is coeval with the discovery of the bad and contempt for it. Instinct and intellect must be suppressed by education. The natural soul is to be replaced with an artificial one.[9]

American culture is experiencing the fruit of years of postmodern and post-truth programming of the mind. This is played out in daily life and not just the classroom, where the answer to every question will find the post-truth theorist opining, instead of defining truth. The consequences of this are already evident, as Barna has discovered in their research: "according to a majority of American adults (57%), knowing what is right or wrong is a matter of personal experience."[10] The people are merely exhibiting what they have been trained to think and do. Jesus established the source of what one says or does in Luke 6:43-45 (NKJV):

---

9. Bloom, *The Closing Of*, 30.

10. "The End of Absolutes: America's New Moral Code," Culture & Media, Barna, May 25, 2016, accessed December 6, 2019, https://www.barna.com/research/the-end-of-absolutes-americas-new-moral-code/.

[43] "For a good tree does not bear bad fruit, nor does a bad tree bear good fruit. [44] For every tree is known by its own fruit. For *men* do not gather figs from thorns, nor do they gather grapes from a bramble bush. [45] A good man out of the good treasure of his heart brings forth good; and an evil man out of the evil treasure of his heart brings forth evil. For out of the abundance of the heart his mouth speaks.

In a post-truth cultural context, how does one decide correctly in matters of moral and ethical significance determined to be right or wrong? Before that, how are matters considered an objective or subjective truth claim in the first place?

An objective truth claim is transcendent. Namely, it is either true or not true, regardless of anyone's opinion. The fact of the matter transcends any agreement or disagreement because it is apart from opinions or feelings. Subjective truth is determined as true, based on a person's feelings or opinions. This is synonymous with post-truth thinking.

If a person says their house is made of wood and brick, this is true or not true, regardless of one's opinion or feelings. It is objectively true, transcendently true.

If another individual says they believe the best houses are only made of wood and brick, then that is subjective or based on their opinion or feeling. It is an opinion because someone may have an entirely different idea as to what kind of materials make the best house, or if newer and better materials and methods prove superior at a later time.

If the claim is made that Jesus is God, then this is also objectively true or not true. If someone agrees or disagrees with that claim it is unimportant and does not change whether or not it is true. The core part of these types of claims is anchored in the person or object, regardless of and unchanged by what anyone thinks about it.

Likewise, if the claim is made that pre-marital sex is morally wrong, it also is an objective truth. It is either true or not true, outside of ourselves and our opinions and experiences. What makes it true or not is dependent on the actual evidence presented to prove it.

Also, if you are of the new idea of tolerance, then you will not accept this ultimate truth claim because it is exclusive and does not permit the opposite to be true. If someone is of the traditional understanding of tolerance, he will permit this to be expressed because he respects another person's right to believe or say it, even if he disagrees.

The evidence for such objective truth claims must still be presented to the post-truth thinker even though they will more than likely bypass or reject this evidence. This is where a person will eventually need to move from *believing that* to *believing in*. At some point, one must trust (put faith in) what the preponderance of evidence points to as objectively true.

Many conclude that the evidence points them to the idea that there is no God and therefore their ideas on what is right and wrong can only be determined by the individual or by the agreed majority of consensus. They then trust in those beliefs and truth claims as the Christian does in theirs. The tension arises in the weightier matters of right and wrong, and of life and death. Will a person's belief and trust in one's own subjective truth claims be sufficient to answer those questions?

This is why a higher, separate, and perfect moral lawgiver is required. Apologist and cold-case detective J. Warner Wallace explains the real question in these matters: "And if we can provide evidence that objective truth claims such as these are a reality in our universe, we must eventually account for such objective, transcendent moral laws. Precisely what kind of transcendent moral lawgiver is required if these kinds of moral laws exist?"[11]

Once we understand that the evidence only proves the moral Lawgiver is the God of the Bible, only then we can clearly see the evidence of what is true and untrue, right and wrong. A great lesson in this is drawn from the life of post-exilic Israel as they had gradually disengaged from the truth in their beliefs and behavior because they had disengaged from the God of truth. There was a remnant, though, who kept the faith in Whom they knew to be true regardless of what they felt or experienced. God then affirmed and rewarded their faith as we see in Malachi 3:16-18,

> [16] Then those who feared the LORD spoke to one another, And the LORD listened and heard *them;* So a book of remembrance was written before Him For those who fear the LORD And who meditate on His name. [17] "They shall be Mine," says the LORD

11. J. Warner Wallace, "Objective Truth Is One Thing, But Objective Moral Truth Is Another," Blog, Cold-Case Christianity, February 4, 2015, accessed December 14, 2019, https://coldcasechristianity.com/writings/objective-truth-is-one-thing-but-objective-moral-truth-is-another/.

of hosts, "On the day that I make them My jewels. And I will spare them as a man spares his own son who serves him." [18] Then you shall again discern Between the righteous and the wicked, between one who serves God And one who does not serve Him.

The Culture of Confusion

Another devastating result of the post-truth system is that it creates confusion. This is the only possible outcome of a relativistic scheme that changes and is based only on feelings and opinions and not on objective, changeless truth. It is a repeat of what God describes in the days of the Judges, "every man did what was right in his own eyes." (Judges 17:6; 21:25)

With this disregard for absolute truth to which all must adhere, we arrive at being a society that reverses right and wrong. What was virtuous is now indecorous. Everything is mercilessly criticized, problematized, and politicized. Murray again expresses the sentiment well, "When we look at our world today and see all the questions being asked amid a culture not truly committed to sound answers, it's hard to imagine a land more confusing."[12]

One of the clearest indicators of this culture of confusion is the shifting sands of what is sexuality and gender. In the state of New York, there are officially thirty-one genders that are recognized and

---

12. Murray, *Saving Truth*, 24.

legally protected.[13] This confusion is affecting our families at an alarming rate.

In the area of gender alone, there is an unprecedented rise in the muddled defining of what is gender. Many do not align their personhood as a man or woman according to their unmistaken biological anatomy they were born with. Today a person identifies as they feel. They can feel they are either a man or woman, or some other self-defined gender identity, or even as a dog[14] or other animals. The negative effects of confusion over this once basic and untouched definition will be unprecedented and distressing in the future of American society as a whole.

One of the most disconcerting post-truth trends is how children are brought into this confusion concerning their humanity and gender by their own parents. In their misguided effort to not impose a gender standard on their children, some parents call their children *theybies*. They raise their children asexually until the child decides which they are or want to be and declare as such to their parents.[15]

13. Elizabeth Harrington, "De Blasio's New York: City Now Defines Gender as Male, Female, 'Or Something Else Entirely'," Issues, Washington Free Beacon, June 1, 2019, accessed December 6, 2019, https://freebeacon.com/issues/de-blasio-nyc-gender/.

14. Susan Donaldson James, "Pittsburgh Man Thinks He's a Dog, Goes By Name 'Boomer,'" ABC News, November 6, 2013, accessed December, 2019, https://abcnews.go.com/Health/pittsburgh-man-thinks-dog-boomer/story?id=20801512.

15. Julie Compton, "'Boy or girl?' Parents raising 'theybies' let kids decide," NBC News, July 19, 2018, accessed December, 2019,

In one standout story of this phenomenon, a single mother in Texas who professes to be a follower of Jesus, is an avid church attendee and Bible reader, and politically conservative, experienced one of her children declare early on that he was not a boy but a girl. After resisting it at first, she eventually became convinced and supportive of her son's early and persistent feelings. She and her transgender son's story became national news during the famous "bathroom bill" battles in Texas in 2016. The mother converted into an advocate for LGBTQ rights and gave public vocal support for the opposition to the bill, which mandated that one can only go to the bathroom of their biological designation on their birth certificate.

Perhaps the most public situation to date representing our post-truth culture's confusion in the area of gender and child-raising occurred in late 2019, with the court battle of a couple and their child. The mother, a pediatrician, believed the child wanted to be a girl, and she had sought counseling and intended to start the chemical and surgical process to accommodate the boy's desire to be a girl. The father called it all a lie, saying the boy has always identified as a boy (which is also his actual biological reality). The jury voted 11-1 in favor of the mother, but the judge nixed that by only restoring joint custody of the child.[16]

https://www.nbcnews.com/feature/nbc-out/boy-or-girl-parents-raising-theybies-let-kids-decide-n891836.

16. Muri Assuncao, "7-year-old in the middle of custody battle between two parents who disagree over child's gender identity," New York Daily News, October 25, 2019, accessed December, 2019, http://www.nydailynews.com/news/national/ny-transgender-child-custody-

In a post-truth society the idea is that if you have clarity or certitude about essential issues, then you are derided and discarded as intolerant and narrow-minded. On the other hand, if you are confused or unclear, then you are considered humble, tolerant, open-minded, virtuous and even celebrated. The discouraging confusion is aptly described by Abdu Murray: "But our demands for truth are so often selective—we want truth when it's convenient or when it supports our point of view. When we look at our world today and see all the questions being asked amid a culture not truly committed to sound answers, it's hard to imagine a land more confusing."[17]

In a truth-based society, when it comes to important issues concerning our humanity, ethics, law, marriage, the family, gender, sexuality, and our faith belief, there is a certainty because of one's openness and compliance to the objective, absolute truths established in God's Word. The answers being bantered about by talking heads across the educational, political and even religious landscapes are not bringing satisfactory answers to these dilemmas. There never will be clarity for the culture entirely until there is a return and restoration to the fundamental absolute truths that God gives to us about who we are and how we can truly live.

To be clear, to return to the traditional Judeo-Christian ethical and moral moorings does not imply that everyone become religious or converts to being Christians. Though not without errors or blemishes, by and large, the American culture functioned successfully

texas-anne-georgulas-jeffrey-younger-20191025-
m6j6m2k5bzfaloqqncbnmipmkm-story.html.

17. Murray, *Saving Truth*, 24.

for over 200 years without confusion in the most fundamental underpinnings of family, morality, faith, and true liberty of the individual and the nation. The traditional parameters based on principles within a literal reading of Scripture gave America a moral authority and exceptionalism to be an example and a liberator of other cultures under oppressive and tyrannical regimes. By moving the goalposts, we have opened a post-truth Pandora's box that is causing a corruption from within that could very well be our downfall.

What Is Freedom?

In post-truth culture, one of the most dominant attitudes is that of demanding one's rights and freedom to be and do as they wish. To suggest any disagreement with the belief and behavior of an individual is considered fascist and attempting to take away one's rights.

Two types of freedoms exist which mankind desires and experiences: negative and positive freedom, as described by Isaiah Berlin. Berlin wrote that *negative freedom* means "... not being interfered with by others. The wider the area of noninterference the wider my freedom."[18] Notwithstanding, there is also another form of freedom and that is what Berlin calls *positive freedom* and characterizes it as "... not freedom from, but freedom to..."[19] God alone is the one who grants the most basic human freedoms from certain things and to do others. Moreover, as our forefathers

18. Isaiah Berlin, *Four Essays on Liberty* (New York: Oxford U.P., 1969), 8.
19. Berlin, *Four Essays on Liberty, 8.*

understood and believed, to government God has delegated the responsibility to protect those God-given freedoms (Rom. 13:1-7) and not act as the sole grantor of them.

One of the confusions that many do not understand is that genuine rights do not come from government or other people. The most basic human rights are defined and bestowed on us by God alone. With the postmodern and post-truth wholesale rejection of God and His laws, individuals with such a type of thinking can only see their freedoms given to them by human government.

The truth is, if there is no objective Lawgiver and laws who give us our fundamental human freedoms, then there is no truly higher law standard; it remains only one's word against the other. In the post-truth mindset, if one perceives and believes there are objective laws derived from a higher Lawgiver, then it remains that there is a divine authority over them. This divine authority that is separate and above man is what he refuses due to his rebellious and sinful nature (Eccl. 9:3; Jer. 17:9; Rom. 1:16-32, 3:10-13).

Abdu Murray explains that the reason why there is this confusion in the area of freedom is that "we have mistaken autonomy for freedom."[20] The idea of negative freedom is to be free from restraints. Positive freedom requires there be certain restraints, for otherwise we are never truly free to be and do what we were always intended as designed by God. Without God's plumb line of those certain restraints, we end up with the post-truth chaos, polarization, and the division we have today in our Western culture. As Murray

20. Murray, *Saving Truth*, 48.

further explains, "freedom becomes chaotic in a system without constraint. Freedom operates at its best within the confines of the truth. Boundaries are foreign to pure autonomy, which means that truth is being sacrificed on autonomy's altar ... When truth is sacrificed as the burnt offering on the altar of autonomy, the resultant smoke chokes the breath out of freedom. Only chaos remains, which ultimately leads to bondage."[21]

The final and only solution to this chaos in the arena of freedom and personal liberty is found in the only One who not only gives the soul freedom, but also is, Himself, that sole true freedom that the world needs: The Lord Jesus Christ. He alone gives any man or woman freedom from sin and freedom to live as God intended. He clearly established this in John 8:32 (NKJV) "And you shall know the truth, and the truth shall make you free," and John 8:36 (NKJV) "Therefore if the Son makes you free, you shall be free indeed."

The Grievance Culture

Post-truth idealists have a utopian goal which promises that, should we all fall in line with their respective mode of thinking and believing, then the world will become a much better, if not more perfect, place to live. The problem is that after decades of such promises by rival belief systems, this has not been the case, and they are worsening the prospects for the peaceful society that all desire to have.

21. Murray, *Saving Truth*, 50.

Intersectionality and critical race theory are the two most significant offenders with respect to belief systems that have only increased the division and strife in America. Within their overlapping spheres are the corrosive ideals of *blackness* versus *whiteness*.

What is blackness? According to historian and professor Dr. Nell Irvin Painter, in an op-ed for the New York Times, says:

> ...whiteness continued to be defined, as before, primarily by what it isn't: blackness... Eliminating the binary definition of whiteness — the toggle between nothingness and awfulness — is essential for a new racial vision that ethical people can share across the color line. Just as race has been reinvented over the centuries, let's repurpose the term "abolitionist" as more than just a hashtag. The "abolition" of white privilege can be an additional component of identity (not a replacement for it), one that embeds social justice in its meaning. Even more, it unifies people of many races.[22]

This definition sounds obscure, but basically, it states that blackness is all that is not whiteness, and vice versa. In other words, whatever is not black, regardless of heritage or cultural ethnicity or skin color, is white. This is a form of reverse racism or racism in its traditional definition.[23] This critical race theory definition of

---

22. Nell Irvin Painter, "What Is Whiteness?," *The New York Times* (June 20, 2015), accessed December 6, 2019,

https://www.nytimes.com/2015/06/21/opinion/sunday/what-is-whiteness.html.

23. racism, *Oxford Advanced Learner's Dictionary*, 8th ed. (n.p.: Oxford University Press, 2013). 1 the unfair treatment of people who belong to a different race;

blackness is rooted in black liberation theology and not pure biblical theology.

Another uninhibited example of such racism within the broader Christian world is seen in an on-stage interview with theologian Ekemini Uwan at the Sparrow Conference, 2019 in Dallas. Here is a section of some of her comments:

> So then when we talk about white identity, then we have to talk about what whiteness is. Well, the reality is that whiteness is rooted in plunder, in theft, in slavery, in enslavement of Africans, genocide of Native Americans, we are sitting on stolen land, if you are in America, we are sitting on stolen land, everywhere in America, this is the reality of land that was stolen from Native Americans and we have to recognize and acknowledge that. It's a power structure, that is what whiteness is, and so that the thing for white women to do is you have to divest from whiteness because what happened was that your ancestors actually made a deliberate choice to rid themselves of their ethnic identity and by doing so they actually stripped Africans in America of their ethnic identity...Because we have to understand something - *whiteness is wicked. It is wicked.* It's rooted in violence, it's rooted in theft, it's rooted in plunder, it's rooted in power, in privilege... The work is to divest from whiteness and the work is also for people of color to divest from whiteness too.[24] (emphasis mine)

violent behaviour towards them, 2 the belief that some races of people are better than others.

24. "Ekemini Uwan Interview by Elizabeth Woodson," (May 2019), accessed December 6, 2019, https://t.co/fgVcDdDqDk.

In addition to the racism of these worldly philosophies masquerading as Christian belief, the overall approach of post-truth only leads to a censorial attitude and action toward those who disagree with them that are not *woke* enough. They brand others who do not comply with their creed, seeking to even cut off their livelihood and reputation in the universities and workplaces. The very ones who profess tolerance suddenly are themselves the intolerant ones. This applies not only to Christians, but also others among the modernists and liberals who now see the danger in the extremism as evidenced in the tactics and takeover in education, media, and politics.

The post-truth activists promoting these divisive theories from inside Christianity are not embodying the Christ-like characteristics that cultivate racial reconciliation, healing, and unity of all races and types of people under the banner of Christ. Instead, they are promoting a form of ethnic hatred and class envy that is Marxian in its essence, which only further deeply divides and destroys communities, families, and churches. The ethnic hatred of these purported representatives of Christianity are pierced to the heart and reprimanded by the very words of Jesus in Luke 18:9-14 (NKJV),

> [9] Also He spoke this parable to some *who trusted in themselves that they were righteous, and despised others*: [10] "Two men went up to the temple to pray, one a Pharisee and the other a tax collector. [11] The Pharisee stood and prayed thus with himself, 'God, I thank You that I am not like other men--extortioners, unjust, adulterers, or even as this tax collector. [12] I fast twice a week; I

give tithes of all that I possess.' [13] And the tax collector, standing afar off, would not so much as raise *his* eyes to heaven, but beat his breast, saying, 'God, be merciful to me a sinner!' [14] I tell you, this man went down to his house justified *rather* than the other; for everyone who exalts himself will be humbled, and he who humbles himself will be exalted." (emphases mine)

The Scriptures tell us that the only way racism and ethnic hatred can be eliminated and healed is through Jesus' death and resurrection, which is the pure and unadulterated Gospel. The words and actions that bring offense to the Gospel are displayed in two pivotal ways: through manipulating the Word of God through worldly philosophies and arguments, and through violating the law of love in and through Jesus Christ to be manifested in His church.

These post-truth religious leaders violate the clear command of Scripture not to allow worldly philosophies into the church that contradict God and His Word, and especially the Gospel. Colossians 2:8 (NKJV) "Beware lest anyone cheat you through philosophy and empty deceit, according to the tradition of men, according to the basic principles of the world, and not according to Christ." James also connects purity of doctrine with the purity of behavior to be Christlike when he says in James 3:13-18 (NKJV):

[13] Who *is* wise and understanding among you? Let him show by good conduct *that* his works *are done* in the meekness of wisdom. [14] But if you have bitter envy and self-seeking in your hearts, do not boast and lie against the truth. [15] This wisdom does not descend from above, but *is* earthly, sensual, demonic. [16] For

where envy and self-seeking *exist,* confusion and every evil thing *are* there. [17] But the wisdom that is from above is first pure, then peaceable, gentle, willing to yield, full of mercy and good fruits, without partiality and without hypocrisy. [18] Now the fruit of righteousness is sown in peace by those who make peace.

These post-truth religious leaders also violate the clear teaching of Scripture that we are to live peaceably with each other in the love of Christ. The Word of God addresses this starting in Galatians 3:28 (NKJV) "There is neither Jew nor Greek, there is neither slave nor free, there is neither male nor female; for you are all one in Christ Jesus." It is also further taught Ephesians 4:1-3 (NKJV) "I, therefore, the prisoner of the Lord, beseech you to walk worthy of the calling with which you were called, with all lowliness and gentleness, with longsuffering, bearing with one another in love, endeavoring to keep the unity of the Spirit in the bond of peace."

When false doctrines are mixed in with true biblical doctrine, behavior changes negatively, and contempt for one another seeps in, which will lead to division engulfing the local church. It also destroys the power and witness of the Gospel to the lost and extinguishes its transforming power of the mind and heart in every area of life. Jude gave a blistering description of such false teachers and then concluded with a directive for all believers regarding the false teachings and teachers in Jude 1:16-23 (NKJV):

These are grumblers, complainers, walking according to their own lusts; and they mouth great swelling *words,* flattering people to gain advantage. But you, beloved, remember the words which were spoken before by the apostles of our Lord Jesus Christ: how they told you that there would be mockers in the last time who would walk according to their own ungodly lusts. These are sensual persons, who cause divisions, not having the Spirit. But you, beloved, building yourselves up on your most holy faith, praying in the Holy Spirit, keep yourselves in the love of God, looking for the mercy of our Lord Jesus Christ unto eternal life. And on some have compassion, making a distinction; but others save with fear, pulling *them* out of the fire, hating even the garment defiled by the flesh.

Post-truth and Morality

Possibly the most visible and most polarizing of post-truth influences is in the area of morality, and specifically concerning the area of life, the human body, and personhood. The challenges in this area by post-truth forces involve large investments of argument, finances, and political pressure.

Since the Supreme Court decision in Roe V. Wade in 1973 striking down a Texas law prohibiting abortion and legalizing it nationwide. The analysis here is not regarding the legality of it but the moral value system (or lack of one) driving it and expanding into other areas concerning the use (or abuse) of the human body.

We see the body being subjected to all kinds of abuse: sexual, physical, abortion, body manipulation, euthanasia, and deviant sexual practices. The human body seems to be both overindulged on one end of the cultural spectrum and exploited, even destroyed, on the other end.

When discussing the overindulgence of the body, it is exemplified in extreme tattooing, medically unnecessary (elective) skin-enhancing injections, breast enhancement, obsessive health and exercise regimens, and instrumentalizing of the body for personal financial gain (e.g., Instagram modeling) and the like.

When discussing the more consequential side of post-truth moral beliefs, we are talking about the abuse or destruction of the body (i.e., killing it). This is demonstrated in the numerous cases of euthanasia of the terminally ill, the aged, the aborting of babies or infanticide in recent years in America and Europe as well.[25]

We have seen the innumerable instances of abortion and the political struggle for and against it. In 2019, after the election being swept by Democrats in the national House of Representatives as well as in state and local races, an immediate push occurred in many places to legalize abortions into the third trimester – and shockingly even after birth (infanticide).[26] In New York, the governor and statehouse stood and applauded their success at passing some of the most

---

25. Peter Cluskey, "Right to euthanasia for people 'tired of life' supported by most Dutch," *Europe, Irish Times*, January 30, 2019, accessed November 19, 2019, https://www.irishtimes.com/news/world/europe/right-to-euthanasia-for-people-tired-of-life-supported-by-most-dutch-1.4088750.

26. Adam Shaw, "Virginia Gov. Northam faces backlash for comments on 3rd-trimester abortion bill: 'Morally repugnant,'" Fox News, January 30, 2019, accessed December 7, 2019, http://www.foxnews.com/politics/va-gov-faces-backlash-for-comments-on-controversial-third-trimester-abortion-bill.

permissive abortion laws in the country.[27] Conversely, other major moves were initiated and successful in other states to limit or even outlaw abortion altogether.[28]

The moral justification for the abuse and destruction of the human body is reinforced by the post-truth manipulation of ethics in the fields of medicine, science, and philosophy. The post-truth views run into direct conflict with the biblical idea of the treatment and use of the physical body. This subtle but powerful shift in influence of the public's thinking and feelings on the subject have been brought to our attention most skillfully by former agnostic and now Christian apologist, Nancy Pearcey, in her book, *Love Thy Body*.

In her book, she relates the story of an article she read by British broadcaster Miranda Sawyer, in which she writes of the conflict between her views as a liberal pro-abortion feminist and being pregnant with her own child. The conclusion she came to is both unorthodox and clever. Dr. Pearcey shows the discovery made in the article:

> Sawyer had run up against the wall of reality—and reality did not fit her ideology. So she began researching the subject, and even produced a documentary. Finally she reached her conclusion: "In

27. Caitlin O'Kane, "New York passes law allowing abortions at any time if mother's health is at risk," CBS News, January 4, 2019, accessed December 7, 2019, https://www.cbsnews.com/news/new-york-passes-abortion-bill-late-term-if-mothers-health-is-at-risk-today-2019-01-23/.

28. Sabrina Tavernise, "'The Time Is Now': States Are Rushing to Restrict Abortion, or to Protect It," *U.S., New York Times*, May 15, 2019, accessed December 7, 2019, http://www.nytimes.com/2019/05/15/us/abortion-laws-2019.html.

the end, I have to agree that life begins at conception. So yes, abortion is ending that life." Then she added, "But perhaps the fact of life isn't what is important. It's whether that life has grown enough . . . to start becoming a person." What has happened here to the concept of the human being? It has been torn in two. If a baby is human life from conception but not a person until some later time, then clearly these are two different things. This is a radically fragmented, fractured, dualistic view of the human being.[29]

The goalposts are moved again in the moral and political battles for a baby's life. The backdrop to this on a national and indeed international level is that medical science is continually widening the ability to support the survivability of a baby outside the womb to as early as 21 weeks.[30] This is on top of the numerous studies through the years, based on scientific and even visual evidence, of the baby being a human life from conception or earlier than 21 weeks. In other words, the scientific facts are not helping the pro-abortion cause.

With the truth pitting itself against the pro-abortion agenda, more in the pro-abortion movement itself are quietly admitting the fetus as a human life, even from conception. They then have opened a new category to determine killing the baby or not. Pearcey uncovers

29. Nancy R. Pearcey, *Love Thy Body: Answering Hard Questions About Life and Sexuality* (Grand Rapids: Baker Books, 2018), 18.

30. A. Pawlowsky, "'Miracle baby,'" Health & Wellness, Today, November 9, 2017, accessed December 7, 2019, https://www.today.com/health/born-21-weeks-she-may-be-most-premature-surviving-baby-t118610.

this by saying, "Thus we have a new category of individual: the human non-person."[31]

This is a typical post-truth act of ignoring the undeniable facts and creating a new truth to fit one's self-developed opinions or feelings to fit a metanarrative that cannot be surrendered. Pearcey expounds on this metanarrative: "This is called personhood theory, and it is an outworking of the fact/value split: To be biologically human is a scientific fact. But to be a person is an ethical concept, defined by what we value. The implication of this two-story view is that simply being human is not enough to qualify for rights."[32] Therefore, until the baby qualifies for personhood, according to their self-made list of qualifications, the baby is just fleshy matter that can be disposed of. The entire post-truth idea is that the body, humanity, and personhood of the individual are separated. As long as they are separated, then the body can be manipulated, abused, or discarded morally and legally.

This dualistic view ultimately collides with the truth of Scripture, which unifies the personhood with their physical body as one intertwined entity with the mind and soul. The biblical Christian view is supported throughout Scripture. In Psalm 139:13-17 (NKJV) the psalmist emotionally pens the words,

> [13] For You formed my inward parts; You covered me in my mother's womb. [14] I will praise You, for I am fearfully *and* wonderfully made; Marvelous are Your works, and *that* my soul

31. Pearcey, *Love Thy Body*, 18.
32. Pearcey, *Love Thy Body*, 19.

knows very well. [15] My frame was not hidden from You, When I was made in secret, *and* skillfully wrought in the lowest parts of the earth. [16] Your eyes saw my substance, being yet unformed. And in Your book they all were written, the days fashioned for me, when *as yet there were* none of them. [17] How precious also are Your thoughts to me, O God! How great is the sum of them!

Again in Genesis 1:26-28, 2:7-8, 15-25, the literal creation story shows that God made us in His image, male and female only, uniquely made to complement each other, which is confirmed by the undeniable reality of the differing, yet interlocking, anatomy of each other.

Furthermore, the evidence of this oneness of body, soul & spirit is seen in the very actions of God the Father with the Son Jesus Christ Himself! The Supreme Being decided to come and be as one of us, human in every way, even into having a biologically fleshly body as a male (Jn. 1:14). He arose in a physical body, though now glorified, in which He could walk, talk, eat and drink, doing so for forty days after His resurrection before literally hundreds of eyewitnesses (Luke 2:1-7; 24:1-53). God continues to reveal His utmost value in the physical human body by also transforming all believers into new and glorified eternal yet physically appearing bodies in eternal heaven one day soon (1 Cor. 15:20-58).

The Christian worldview alone maintains the higher value and respect for the human body as one with the person. This oneness of personhood is a gift of God made in His image and it impacts all the issues pertaining to it, such as gender, sexuality, care, appearance, and life and death. The Word of God illuminates our understanding of not only our soul and spirit, but also the body, in a unity managed together under the laws and instruction of God, who is Maker and Lord of all.

Chapter 14

The Hope of the Gospel in a Post-truth World

So what kind of a future and world does post-truth lead us to? The American alternative rock group Matchbox Twenty wrote a song whose lyrics and chorus express the despair that comes from a world without the only real truth:

> It's gone gone, baby it's all gone
> There is no one on the corner and there's no one at home
> It was cool cool, it was just all cool
> Now it's over for me, and it's over for you
> Well its gone gone, baby it's all gone

There is no one on the corner and there's no one at home

Well it was cool cool, it was just all cool

Now it's over for me, and it's over for you

But I believe the world is burning to the ground

Oh well, I guess we're gonna find out

Let's see how far we've come

Let's see how far we've come

Well I, believe, it all, is coming to an end

Oh well, I guess, we're gonna pretend,

Let's see how far we've come

Let's see how far we've come[1]

Abdu Murray notes that "A post-truth culture that elevates feelings over facts gives us only half the picture. And in being half right, it's all wrong."[2] This is largely the reason post-truth misconceptions leave us lost and without hope. If there is no truth, then we are left without parameters within which to live correctly. Without truth, there is no light to show us through and out of the darkness. Without the truth, there is no higher ground on which to stand firmly and safely while the world surrounds us with storm-tossed waves of lies ready to engulf us. The truth provides clarity in the chaos. Why? Because without it, each person becomes a law unto themselves. Self-determined truth claims always pull us into a never-ending labyrinth in which we can't ever find the escape door to final Truth (Judges 17:6, 21:25).

1. Rob Thomas et al., *How Far We've Come* (n.p.: Sony/ATV Music Publishing LLC, 2007).
2. Murray, *Saving Truth*, 224.

Though an atheist, philosopher Julian Baggini aptly pinpoints the real problem of this self-guided search for truth when he says, "Our problem is not primarily with what truth means but how and by whom truth is established."[3] So then how and by whom is the Truth established?

The Truth we are really looking for is not a carefully crafted belief system, creed, or ritual. The Truth is first and foremost a Person who is the Lord Jesus Christ, the Son of God. In John 14:6 Jesus established by whom the truth is established. Jesus revealed that the truth is embodied in the very Person of the incarnate God Himself, Jesus: "I am the way, *the truth*, and the life. No one comes to the Father except through Me." (emphasis mine)

How do we know He is the only abiding Truth for everyone? We know God and what He says are altogether the Truth because it is backed up by His sinless character and the finished work of the cross and empty tomb. J.I Packer in his classic book, Knowing God, explains this well:

> But the claim of the word of God upon us does not depend merely upon our relationship to him as creatures and subjects. We are to believe and obey it, not only because he tells us to, but also, and primarily, because it is a true word. Its author is "the God of truth" (Ps 31:5; Is 65:16), "abundant in . . . truth" (Ex 34:6 KJV); his "truth reacheth unto the clouds" (Ps 108:4 KJV; compare 57:10)—that is, it is universal and limitless. Therefore his "word is truth" (Jn 17:17). "All your words are true" (Ps

3. Baggini, *A Short History*, Location 68.

119:160). "Thou art God, and thy words are true" (2 Sam 7:28 RSV). Truth in the Bible is a quality of persons primarily, and of propositions only secondarily. It means stability, reliability, firmness, trustworthiness, the quality of a person who is entirely self-consistent, sincere, realistic, undeceived. God is such a person: truth, in this sense, is his nature, and he has not got it in him to be anything else.[4]

His truth is dependent on the righteous and holy character of God, as seen in Jesus. Frank Turek points out the scriptural evidence for His perfect, sinless character:

> Jesus himself said, "Which one of you convicts Me of sin" (John 8:46, NASB)? Moreover, his disciples, who spent three years with him day and night, claimed that Jesus was sinless: Peter characterized Jesus as an "unblemished and spotless" lamb (1 Pet. 1:19, NASB) "who committed no sin, nor was any deceit found in His mouth" (1 Pet. 2:22, NASB). John said of Christ, "in Him there is no sin" (1 John 3:5, NASB). Paul wrote that Jesus "knew no sin" (2 Cor. 5:21, NASB). The writer of Hebrews made the same point by claiming that Jesus was "without sin" (Heb. 4:15, NASB).[5]

Post-truth relies almost entirely on feelings, yet this does not mean that feelings are not necessary when it comes to God's Truth. To the contrary, we do not want to just not know the truth but to feel it and experience it as well. If we have only truth as factual

4. J. I. Packer, *Knowing God* (Downers Grove, Ill: InterVarsity Press, 1973), 113.
5. Geisler and Turek, *I Don't Have Enough*, 348.

information, then we can make it be dry and lifeless lecture material. If we have only love, then we eventually end up with only mushy sentimentalism or worse.

God brings both together in One, Jesus, because He is truth (Jn. 14:6) and He is love (1 Jn. 4:8, 16). Once again, Abdu Murray explains this articulately:

> We don't need something to make us alive. We need someone. In Christ truth and personal feelings converge. Both are important. In our zeal for autonomy, we've fallen into confusion by elevating personal feelings above truth. But we have to be careful not to succumb to the equally confused idea that cold hard facts alone will liberate us. Truth has to be personal if it is to touch our minds and hearts.[6]

The truth of God is personal because it is Jesus, the personal God who feels. He invades our hearts, minds, and soul with His truth, so we not only know it but feel it deep within. His truth does this within us because through it He brings us life. In responding to the temptation of Satan against Him, Jesus responded to the temptation of Satan in Matthew 4:4 and Luke 4:4: "But He answered and said, "It is written, 'Man shall not live by bread alone, but by every word that proceeds from the mouth of God.'"

Jesus denounced the religious authorities, such as the Pharisees, for contorting and making His words lifeless. We see this in his vehement rebuke in Matthew 23:23: "Woe to you, scribes and Pharisees, hypocrites! For you pay tithe of mint and anise and

6. Murray, *Saving Truth*, 223.

cummin and have neglected the weightier *matters* of the law: justice and mercy and faith. These you ought to have done, without leaving the others undone." and again in John 6:63, "It is the Spirit who gives life; the flesh profits nothing. The words that I speak to you are spirit, and *they* are life."

If the truth of the Word of God is reduced to just another self-serving man-centered body of beliefs, then its rightful offense to the sinful conscience of mankind cannot bring the godly repentance and faith that follows it unto salvation (Rom. 1:16).

In 2 Corinthians 4:2 (NKJV) Paul the apostle wrote this under inspiration of God the Holy Spirit: "But we have renounced the hidden things of shame, not walking in craftiness nor handling the word of God deceitfully, but by manifestation of the truth commending ourselves to every man's conscience in the sight of God."

This verse speaks so directly of how we as the church are to fight the battle we face in our post-truth world, both within the church and in the world. Here and throughout the New Testament, we are instructed to maintain the integrity of the truth through three endeavors: (1) we must be faithful in protecting and preserving the veracity of the written Word, (2) we must protect and preserve the integrity of the truth of God by living according to the truth of God, and (3) we must reach others with the truth of God by being and showing the love of Jesus to them. We are commanded to literally practice what we preach if the Word of God is to have any convicting and transformative impact on our own life as well as on the minds and hearts of unsaved people.

In carrying out the first task, we must make sure we protect the Word's integrity and meaning. Jude, led by the Holy Spirit, turned the theme of his God-inspired letter to tell us simply and directly in Jude verses 3 and 4,

> Beloved, while I was very diligent to write to you concerning our common salvation, I found it necessary to write to you exhorting you to contend earnestly for the faith which was once for all delivered to the saints. For certain men have crept in unnoticed, who long ago were marked out for this condemnation, ungodly men, who turn the grace of our God into lewdness and deny the only Lord God and our Lord Jesus Christ.

When Jude writes for us to contend for *the faith*, he is referring not to salvation faith or faith for living, but rather the body of belief that God has given us in the written record of God. We are to be set to defend its integrity in translation, interpretation, and application (2 Jn. Vv. 7-11). We are also to defend it by rebuking those who would dishonorably change it through manipulation or repudiation (1 Jn. 4:1; Rev. 22:6-7, 18-19). We are also commanded to preserve and protect its integrity by faithfully expounding its words as they are intended (2 Tim. 2:15, 3:16). We do this through preaching and teaching (2 Tim. 4:2; Heb. 4:12) and through effectively making disciples of Jesus who in turn will make more disciples of Jesus (Mat. 28:18; 2 Tim. 2:2).

We have discussed much about the first endeavor, which is to safeguard the purity of the very words and teachings of the Scriptures. The second one is that we are upbraided to be examples of the truth of God in our daily living as faith communities of the Lord Jesus Christ (Ps. 119:11; Mat. 5:16; Jn. 13:35; Gal. 2:6-7; Phil. 1:20; 1 Pet. 2:1-2; 3 Jn. V. 11-12). To this latter effort of being living proof of the Gospel truth, Nancy Pearcey adeptly writes,

> "Christians must be prepared to minister to the wounded, the refugees of the secular moral revolution whose lives have been wrecked by its false promises of freedom and autonomy. When people are persuaded that they are ultimately disconnected, atomistic selves, their relationships will grow fragile and fragmented. Those around us will increasingly suffer insecurity and loneliness. The new polarization can be an opportunity for Christian communities to become safe havens where people witness the beauty of relationships reflecting God's own commitment and faithfulness.[7]

In fulfilling the third task of loving others as Jesus did, we are acting in the opposite way of the post-truth world. It is the way we extend the love of Christ even in disputations and challenges to truth and faith.

As noted before, under its various ideologies, the frequent post-truth treatment of others is to attack them personally. The reason for this is the post-truth deficiency of possessing sound, historical, scholarly, or proven foundation of truth principles. Without this type

7. Pearcey, *Love Thy Body*, 264.

of foundation post-truth advocates are incapable of articulating successful arguments against objective truth-based principles and beliefs. To make up for such deficiency, post-truth influencers and activists can only usually resort to attacking the character or wisdom of the individual. This rhetorical ploy was employed by the late atheist-turned-Christian-apologist C.S. Lewis as *Bulverism*:

> In other words, you must show that a man is wrong before you start explaining why he is wrong. The modern method is to assume without discussion that he is wrong and then distract his attention from this (the only real issue) by busily explaining how he became so silly. In the course of the last fifteen years I have found this vice so common that I have had to invent a name for it. I call it Bulverism. Some day I am going to write the biography of its imaginary inventor, Ezekiel Bulver, whose destiny was determined at the age of five when he heard his mother say to his father — who had been maintaining that two sides of a triangle were together greater than the third — 'Oh you say that because you are a man.' 'At that moment', E. Bulver assures us, 'there flashed across my opening mind the great truth that refutation is no necessary part of argument. Assume that your opponent is wrong, and then explain his error, and the world will be at your feet.[8]

The attack of the person themselves may get attention and push the truth-thinker back on their heels because they are forced and distracted for the moment to defend their very own reputation.

8. C.S. Lewis, *God in the Dock*, ed. Walter Hoope, kindle ed., Fount paperbacks (Grand Rapids: William B. Eerdmans, 1970), Location 3305.

Nonetheless, this approach is short-lived, and eventually, evidence and facts will be required, and the argument rises or falls on that alone in the end.

So how does the believer respond biblically and effectively to a post-truth world? In response to the concerns of how the post-truth society will react to our responses of truth, we need to remember to tamper down our expectations of how they will respond to biblical absolute truth and deliver the truth and love of Jesus to where it needs to go regardless of the reactions. Phil Mobley puts it this way:

> Scripture warns us to manage our expectations about the outcome of truth-telling. The truth is uncomfortable to a world that has exchanged it for a lie. Even Christian believers are still prone to hide from truth. Paul feared that the Galatians would view him as an enemy when he offered truth intended to correct their belief and practice (Galatians 4:16). Yet the likelihood of conflict is no reason to withhold truth. Moreover, to do so would be unloving — no one benefits from persisting in a false reality.[9]

Ravi Zacharias, perhaps Christianity's greatest modern-day apologist, has said often that "I always bear in mind that behind every question is a questioner."[10] Every question (or even accusation) is

---

9. Phil Mobley, "Post-truth (And Consequences)," In The World, Online Magazine of the Presbyterian Church of America-byFaith, November 27, 2018, accessed August 20, 2019, https://dictionary.cambridge.org/us/dictionary/english/post-truth.

10. Ravi Zacharias, "Deep Questions," Think Again, RZIM, accessed December 5, 2019, https://www.rzim.org/read/just-thinking-magazine/think-again-deep-questions.

made by a person, one for which Jesus died and rose again, and that needs the very Savior that the person rejects.

The Apostle Peter was himself publicly confronted by Paul for compromising Jesus' truth for cultural acceptance (Gal. 2:11-14). Later, Peter then penned these instructions to us in 1 Peter 3:15 (ESV):

> But even if you should suffer for righteousness' sake, you will be blessed. Have no fear of them, nor be troubled, but in your hearts honor Christ the Lord as holy, always being prepared to make a defense to anyone who asks you for a reason for the hope that is in you; yet do it with gentleness and respect, having a good conscience, so that, when you are slandered, those who revile your good behavior in Christ may be put to shame.

Our response is to give the best answer as a defense of the Gospel, with godly gentleness and respect for the questioner. The Christian's truth-based response is to be in "gentleness and respect" (1 Pet. 3:15 [ESV]). How we respond can speak volumes more of Jesus and the Gospel than the actual words themselves.

These monumental tasks of defending the truth, living the truth, and loving others in the truth, have been given by God and are not just for us as individuals. We are a part of His worldwide family, the church, and in particular, the local church. We are to be the church of Jesus Christ committed to these tasks with each other in the church and also amongst our friends, family, and community in the world (Mat. 5:16, 16:18; Eph. 4:11-16; 1 Pet. 2:12, 15).

It is vital to also remember that these sacred responsibilities must be carried out not only among the adults but, even more importantly, to the youth of our culture. This is intrinsically true of the mandate of Jesus to take the Gospel to everyone worldwide and to teach all the truth of Scripture (Mat. 28:19; Luke 18:16).

It is also critical to reach our youth with His truth because of the onslaught of post-truth immersion of our children and teenagers. The alarming rate of damage caused by post-truth in the individual and the culture is not only being felt now, but will also only increase generationally. The battle for the minds and hearts is constant and one in which the devil and sinful mankind do not relent in carrying out. John Dickerson reminds us of the task of leading the young into God's truth in the midst of the post-truth world:

> The Post-Truth worldview is so pervasive, so slippery, so all-encompassing in media, entertainment, and cultural assumptions, that we cannot assume our Christian children will emerge into adulthood with a Truth-Based, Christian view of reality. Quite the opposite. We must assume that, short of overwhelming intentional effort and concerted prayer, our children will absorb the spirit of this age and the Post-Truth ideology that accompanies it. Christianity is at its best when it is an overtly countercultural movement. And this is now the position in which we find ourselves—if we're honest about the realities around us. We must begin thinking, behaving, and planning accordingly. If we want our children and grandchildren to be among the one-third who retain the faith beyond age twenty-nine, we must equip them with an intellectual and

spiritual foundation of such reinforced fortitude as to stand unweathered through a lifelong storm of oppression.[11]

The training up of our children (Prov. 22:6) will only happen when husbands and wives, fathers and mothers, believe and live the commands and principles of God and faithfully love and follow Jesus first in their own lives. In teaching the biblical values to our children and youth, it will be caught more than taught. The local church is to be the supporting community to the family and the place where the family can receive instruction and guidance through the Word lived out in others' lives around them there.

11. Dickerson, *Hope of Nations*, 211.

Chapter 15

Conclusion: The Truth Will Overcome

Post-truth, in reality, is not new. It first reared its ugly head thousands of years ago in the Garden of Eden when the serpent (Satan) tempted Eve and, in turn, Adam, our representative head. Satan caused them to doubt God's truth and to believe a lie masquerading as truth. This post-truth tactic is still his tool today: ignore or discard the known truth and replace it with false belief.

Several thousand years later, God's prophet at the time was Jeremiah, who stood in the Temple courtyard and delivered a stinging rebuke from God to the people of Judah in Jeremiah 9:3-9 (NKJV),

³ "And like their bow they have bent their tongues for lies. They are not valiant for the truth on the earth. For they proceed from evil to evil, and they do not know Me," says the LORD. ⁴ "Everyone take heed to his neighbor, and do not trust any brother; For every brother will utterly supplant, and every neighbor will walk with slanderers. ⁵ Everyone will deceive his neighbor, and will not speak the truth; They have taught their tongue to speak lies; They weary themselves to commit iniquity. ⁶ Your dwelling place is in the midst of deceit; Through deceit they refuse to know Me," says the LORD. ⁷ Therefore thus says the LORD of hosts: "Behold, I will refine them and try them; For how shall I deal with the daughter of My people? ⁸ Their tongue *is* an arrow shot out; It speaks deceit; *One* speaks peaceably to his neighbor with his mouth, but in his heart he lies in wait. ⁹ Shall I not punish them for these things?" says the LORD. "Shall I not avenge Myself on such a nation as this?"

The truth about the lie is explained directly by these warnings Paul gives us in Ephesians 5:6 (NKJV) "Let no one deceive you with empty words, for because of these things the wrath of God comes upon the sons of disobedience." and also in Colossians 2:8 (NKJV), "Beware lest anyone cheat you through philosophy and empty deceit, according to the tradition of men, according to the basic principles of the world, and not according to Christ." (emphases mine)

The forces of post-truth create the ideologies of empty deceit due to three things: One is the need to belong, to feel accepted and known, the second is anger which grows out of the feeling that one has been denied what they deserve, and the third is pride. Whether one perceives themselves as inferior or as powerful, they will feel the need to exalt themselves and control outcomes and people. The third is the core motivation of pride, the original sin and the most heinous to God, as demonstrated initially by Lucifer (afterward, Satan; Is. 14:12-14).

Satan continues to exploit this throughout the ages to destroy those who believe in God and to take what he feels is his rightful throne over God. Today the devil has simply played to man's lust for pride and power through an old tool with new clothes on, and that, today, is post-truth.

We, as believers, are not to buy into the lies of the devil as manifested in the modern fake ideals of intersectionality, critical race theory, socialism or any other number of belief systems and movements inseminated with lies. At the same time, we are urged to reach others with the Good News of Jesus Christ, the only Truth and Light that alone can rescue us from this present darkness.

In John 18:36-38 (NKJV) we find Jesus about to be condemned by Pontius Pilate before the whipped-up crowds who wanted Him crucified. In John 18:37, Jesus told him, "...For this cause I was born, and for this cause I have come into the world, that I should bear witness to the truth. Everyone who is of the truth hears My voice." Then, in John 18:38, we read Pilate's smirky retort, "What is truth?" Just as in the case of Pilate, we cannot pretend that just because we tell someone that Jesus is and says the only Truth, that the world will respond positively and warmly. We must expect that they will mostly respond in any and every evil way (John 16:23; 18:15-23).

Unfortunately, many times Christians also often boast of having all the answers, causing rejection of His truth. Perhaps the more volatile reactions to God's truth is due to the hypocrisy of a Christian whose life does not reflect the truth that his lips profess. Nevertheless, we are to be representatives of the truth, to be truth-bearers of God, to the best of our ability.

We do not have to be eloquent scholars and teachers to be convincing witnesses of the Gospel. In one instance, Peter and John were placed before all the adversarial Jewish religious leaders and rulers and spoke God's truth to them. In Acts 4:13, their dumbfounded response to these apostles is recorded, "Now when they saw the boldness of Peter and John and perceived that they were uneducated and untrained men, they marveled. And they realized that they had been with Jesus." When we live in an evidential way that shows we are walking with Jesus, it too gives us His power to bring the conviction and hope of God to others whose hearts are open to it (Rom. 1:16; Acts 1:8).

We must remember that the truth of God is not a truth that is merely equal to, or competing with, all other manmade truth claims. The truth of God stands supremely apart and above any and all worldly philosophies. The high preeminence of His truth is due to His preeminence as resurrected Savior and Lord. Due to this preeminence, it gives distinct advantages to believers that the false ideas of the world cannot produce.

One of those advantages is that the truth is knowable. Though we may not understand it all, He has shown us all things we need to know for this life's experience (Rom. 11:33-36; 2 Pet. 1:3). Through His Word and His Spirit within us, we get a clear picture of all the issues that post-truth tries to confuse and destroy such as God, redemption, eternity, gender, sexuality, sex, family, marriage, the body, race, creation, science, morality, right and wrong, reward, judgment, justice, dignity, value, freedom, the world, evil and suffering, treatment of others, true tolerance and respect for others, even if they don't agree with us, knowledge, love, and so much more. This is an enormous privilege we are given by God that unsaved persons do not have, nor can they have (John 15:26, 16:7-15; 1 Cor. 2:7-14).

Another advantage is the utmost confidence we can have about His truth because of His fulfilled promises and prophecies (Joshua 21:45; Acts 2:29-36; 1 Jn. 1:1-4). Not only does the evidence from within the Word of God confirm this repeatedly, but also the embarrassment of riches that we have in the numerous external evidences confirming fulfillment as well.

One other advantage is that the truth of God will always remain. It cannot be changed, blotted out, burned away, or obliterated from existing, though many have tried. It is unchangeable and immutable forever (Ps. 119:160; Mat. 5:18; 1 Pet. 1:25).

The next advantage is that we can read the end of the Book and discover that the Truth wins! The victory is in Christ and His blessed Gospel alone (Rev. 21:1-6, 22:1-7)! So, for now, we have the onerous, yet doable, task of knowing and living the truth in our lives. We have a mission to proclaim the Gospel truth to the world in this post-truth age. In his book, *The Other Worldview*, author Peter Jones reminds us of how we can face the challenge of holding forth the Truth in the pace of a post-truth world:

> ...we must ask God to show us how to speak his truth faithfully and courageously in the difficult days ahead. Do not be surprised: Jesus said he "came not to be served but to serve, and to give his life as a ransom for many" (Mark 10: 45). He calls us to take up that same cross and follow him. Indeed, the time is coming when "all who desire to live a godly life in Christ Jesus will be persecuted" (2 Tim 3: 12). Without the transformative power of the gospel, we will lack courage, and our efforts will be in vain.[1]

We are not left without hope in this post-truth world. We have been given the responsibility and privilege to be the hope and truth-bearers of the One who is the only Truth, Jesus Christ, the Son of God. He proved and secured it forever with His sinless life, death and literal bodily resurrection as foretold in the Scriptures and by Jesus Himself (1 Cor. 15:1-4). He is eternal and so His truth is eternal. His truth is light because He is the light (John 1:4-9). Let us then speak, live and reflect His Truth and Light in the love of Christ. His hope never dies because His truth never dies, and this is true because He is alive forevermore!

1 Peter Jones, *The Other Worldview: Exposing Christianity's Greatest Threat* (Bellingham, WA: Kirkdale Press, 2015), Location 3743.

Bibliography

"Ad Hominem." *Merriam-Webster Dictionary*, Accessed December 16, 2019. https://www.merriam-webster.com/dictionary/ad%20hominem.

Adams, Maurianne, Lee Anne Bell, Diane J. Goodman, and Khyati Y. Joshi. *Teaching for Diversity and Social Justice*. Third Edition ed. New York: Routledge, 2016.

Baggini, Julian. *A Short History of Truth*. Kindle ed. London: Quercus Editions Ltd, 2017.

———. A Short History of Truth. Kindle Edition ed., Locations 99–102. London: Quercus Publishing, 2017.

Berlin, Isaiah. *Four Essays on Liberty.* Oxford paperbacks 116, 118–72. New York: Oxford U.P., 1969.

Bloom, Allan. *The Closing of the American Mind.* New York, N.Y: Simon and Schuster, 1987.

Breese, Dave. *Seven Men Who Rule the World from the Grave.* Chicago: Moody Press, 1990.

Cairns, Earle E. *Christianity Through the Centuries: A History of the Christian Church.* 3rd ed. Grand Rapids: MI: Zondervan, 1996.

Cambridge Dictionary s.v. "Post-truth." Accessed August 20, 2019. https://dictionary.cambridge.org/us/dictionary/english/post-truth.

Carroll, Lewis. *Through the Looking Glass.* EPub ed. Toronto, Ontario, Canada: Harper Perennial Classics, 2015.

Carson, D.A. Becoming Conversant with the Emerging Church. Kindle Edition ed. Grand Rapids: Zondervan, 2005.

———, ed.. Telling the Truth: Evangelizing Postmoderns. Kindle ed. Grand Rapids, Mich: Zondervan, 2000.

Crenshaw, Kimberlé. "Demarginalizing the Intersection of Race and Sex:." *University of Chicago Legal Forum* 1989, no. 1.

———. "Demarginalizing the Intersection of Race and Sex: A Black Feminist Critique of Antidiscrimination Doctrine, Feminist Theory and Antiracist Politics." *University of Chicago Legal Forum* 1989, no. 1.

d'Ancona, Matthew. Post Truth: The New War on Truth and How to Fight Back. London: Ebury Press, 2017.

Dawkins, Richard. *The Blind Watchmaker*. New York: W.W. Nortonamp and Company, 1987.

"Equity." *Lexico*, Accessed October 7, 2019. http://www.lexico.com/en/definition/equity.

Darwall, Rupert. *Green Tyranny: Exposing the Totalitarian Roots of the Climate Industrial Complex*. New York: Encounter Books, 2017.

Dylan, Bob. "Ya Gotta Serve Somebody." In *Slow Train Coming*. New York: Columbia, 1979.

Erete, Sheena. "Demarginalizing the Intersection of Race and Sex:." *ACM INteractions Magazine* 25, no. 3 (May-June 2018): 66–69. Accessed October 7, 2019. http://dx.doi.org/10.1145/3194349.

Feldman, Stephen M. American Legal Thought From Premodernism to Postmodernism. Locations 246-247 ed. New York: Oxford University Press, 2000.

Ferrigon, Phillip. "Person-First Language Vs. Identity-First Language: An Examination of the Gains and Drawbacks of Disability Language in Society." *Journal of Teaching Disability Studies* (January 2019). Accessed November 6, 2019. https://jtds.commons.gc.cuny.edu/person-first-language-vs-identity-first-language-an-examination-of-the-gains-and-drawbacks-of-disability-language-in-society/.

Grace Ji-Sun Kim, and Susan M. Shaw. *Intersectional Theology: An Introductory Guide*. Kindle ed. Minneapolis, MN: Fortress Press, 2018.

Han, Diego. "From Postmodernity to a Post-Truth Society." Journal of Comparative Studies (2018).

Keyes, Ralph. The post-truth Era: Dishonesty and Deception in Contemporary Life. New York: St. Martin's Press, 2004.

Kreitner, Richard. "Consequences: What a 25-Year-Old Essay Tells Us About the Current Moment." Nation, November 30, 2016. Accessed January 5, 2019. http://www.thenation.com/article/post-truth-and-its-consequences-what-a-25-year-old-essay-tells-us-about-the-current-moment/.

Dickerson, John S. Hope of Nations: Standing Strong in a Post-truth, Post-Christian World. Kindle ed. Grand Rapids, Michigan: Zondervan, 2018.

Garofolo, Steven. Right for You, but Not for Me: A Response to Moral Relativism. Kindle ed. Charlotte, NC: TriedStone Publishing Company, 2013.

Hicks, Stephen R. C. Explaining Postmodernism. Expanded Kindle Edition ed. N.p.: Ockham's Razor Publishing, 2014.

Hicks, Stephen R. C. *Explaining Postmodernism*. Expanded Kindle Edition ed. N.p.: Ockham's Razor Publishing, 2014.

———King, & Claude. Experiencing God: How to Live the Full Adventure of Knowing and Doing the Will of God. Rev. and expand ed. Nashville, Tenn: Broadman & Holman Publishers, 1994.

Lutzer, Erwin W. Who Are You to Judge?: Learning to Distinguish between Truths, Half-truths, and Lies. Chicago: Moody Press, 2002.

McCallum, Dennis, ed. The Death of Truth. Minneapolis, Minn: Bethany House Publishers, 1996.

McIntyre, Lee. Post-Truth. Kindle ed. The MIT Press Essential Knowledge Series. Cambridge, MA: MIT Press, 2018.

Carson, D. A. *Becoming Conversant with the Emerging Church: Understanding a Movement and Its Implications*. Kindle ed. Grand Rapids, Mich: Zondervan, 2005.

Evans, C. Stephen. *A History of Western Philosophy: From the Pre-Socratics to Postmodernism*. Kindle ed. Downers Grove: InterVarsity Press, 2018.

Forstenzer, Joshua. *Something Has Cracked: Post-Truth*. Edited by Tony Saich. Ash Center Occasional Papers Series. University of Sheffield (UK): Ash Center for Democratic Governance and Innovation-Harvard Kenedy School, 2018.

Geisler, Norman L., and Frank Turek. *I Don't Have Enough Faith to Be an Atheist*. Wheaton, IL: Crossway, 2004.

Grace Ji-Sun Kim, and Susan M. Shaw. "Biography as Intersectional Theology." In *Intersectional Theology: An Introductory Guide*. Kindle ed. Minneapolis, MN: Fortress Press, 2018.

Hooks, Bell. *Teaching to Transgress: Education as the Practice of Freedom*. New York: Routledge, 1994.

Kimball, Roger. *The Long March: How the Cultural Revolution of the 1960s Changed America*. San Francisco: Encounter Books, 2000.

Lazer, David M. J. et al. "The Science of Fake News." *Science* 359, no. 6380 (March 2018): 1094–96. Accessed August 13, 2019. http://science.sciencemag.org/content/359/6380/1094.

Lemke, Steve W. *"Hellenism."* Edited by Chad Brand. Holman Illustrated Bible Dictionary ed. Nashville: Holman Bible Publishers, 2003.

———. *"Hellenism."* Edited by Chad Brand. Holman Illustrated Bible Dictionary ed. Nashville: Holman Bible Publishers, 2003.

———. *Hellenism.* Edited by Chad Brand. Holman Illustrated Bible Dictionary ed. Nashville: Holman Bible Publishers, 2003.

———. ""Hellenism." In *Holman Illustrated Bible Dictionary*, edited by Chad Brand. Nashville: Holman Bible Publishers, 2003.

Lexico. "s.v. Intersectionality." Accessed October 7, 2019. http://www.lexico.com/en/definition/intersectionality.

"Materialism." *Merriam-Webster Dictionary*, Accessed December 9, 2019. https://www.merriam-webster.com/dictionary/materialism.

Lewis, C.S. *God in the Dock.* Edited by Walter Hoope. Kindle ed. Fount paperbacks. Grand Rapids: William B. Eerdmans, 1970.

Merriam-Webster, Inc. *Merriam-Webster's Dictionary and Thesaurus.* Springfield, Massachusetts: Merriam-Webster, Incorporated, 2009.

———. *Webster's new Explorer Dictionary and Thesaurus.* Springfield, Mass: Federal Street Press, 2009.

Mohler, Albert. "Part III Ideas Have Consequences: Critical race theory and Intersectionality in the News from the Southern Baptist Convention." *The Briefing* (June 2019). Accessed December 13, 2019. https://albertmohler.com/2019/06/14/briefing-6-14-19.

Moreland, J. P. *Scientism and Secularism: Learning to Respond to a Dangerous Ideology*. Wheaton, IL: Crossway, 2018.

Murray, Abdu. Saving Truth: Finding Meaning & Clarity in a Post-truth World. Grand Rapids, Michigan: Zondervan, 2018.

Nickerson, Raymond S. "Confirmation Bias: A Ubiquitous Phenomenon in Many Guises." *Review of General Psychology* 2, no. 2 (1998): 175–220. Accessed September 3, 2019. http://psy2.ucsd.edu/ mckenzie/nickersonConfirmationBias.pdf.

Osborne, Grant R. ""Hellenism." In *Baker Encyclopedia of the Bible*, edited by Didier Fassin. Grand Rapids, MI: Baker Book House, 1988.

Patricia Hill Collins. *Intersectionality as Critical Social Theory*. Kindle ed., Location 5880. Durham: Duke University Press, 2019.

———, and Sirma Bilge. *Intersectionality*. 2nd ed. Key concepts. Medford, MA: Polity Press, 2020.

DiAngelo, Robin. "White Fragility." *International Journal of Critical Pedagogy* 3, no. 3 (2011): 54–70. Accessed November 11, 2019. http://libjournal.uncg.edu/ijcp/article/viewFile/249/116.

Phillips, G., W. Brown, and J. Stonestreet. "Theism: The World from God's Hands." In *Making Sense of Your World*. Second edition ed. Salem, WI: Sheffield Publishing Company, 2008.

Potter, Beverly A., and Mark J. Estren. Question Authority to Think for Yourself. Kindle ed. Oakland, CA: Ronin Publishing,, 2012.

Pearcey, Nancy. *Finding Truth: 5 Principles for Unmasking Atheism, Secularism, and Other God Substitutes*. Kindle ed. Colorado Springs, CO: David C. Cook, 2015.

———. *Love Thy Body*. Kindle ed. Grand Rapids: Baker Books, 2018, November 9, 2017.

———. "Health & Wellness." In *Miracle Baby.* Kindle ed. Colorado Springs, CO: Today, 2015, November 9, 2017.

———. "Health & Wellness." In *Miracle Baby.* Kindle ed., 19–20. Colorado Springs, CO: Today, 2015, November 9, 2017.

———. "Health & Wellness." In *Miracle Baby.* Kindle ed., 19–20. Colorado Springs, CO: Today, 2015, November 9, 2017.

———. "Health & Wellness." In *Miracle Baby.* Kindle ed. Colorado Springs, CO: Today, 2015, November 9, 2017.

Potter, Beverly A., and Mark J. Estren. *Question Authority to Think for Yourself.* Kindle ed. Oakland, CA: Ronin Publishing,, 2012.

Ruse, Michael. "Is Evolution a Secular Religion?" *Science* 299, no. 5612 (March 2003). Accessed December 11, 2019. http://dx.doi.org/10.1126/science.1082968.

———Singer, Margot, and Nicole Walker, eds. *Bending Genre: Essays on Creative Nonfiction.* New York: Bloomsbury, 2013.

Tesich, Steve. "A Government of Lies." Free Library, January 6, 1992. Accessed October 1, 2018. https://www.thefreelibrary.com/A+government+of+lies.-a011665982.

Thompson, Nicholas. "Nuclear War and Nuclear Fear in the 1970's and 1980's." *Journal of Contemporary History* 46, no. 1 (2011): 136–49.

Turek, Frank. *Stealing from God: Why Atheists Need God to Make Their Case.* Colorado Springs: NavPress, 2014.

"What's in a name? Weather, global warming and climate change." climate.nasa.gov. https://climate.nasa.gov/resources/global-warming/.

"What's in a name? Weather, global warming and climate change." climate.nasa.gov. Accessed August 8, 2019. https://climate.nasa.gov/resources/global-warming/.

Tigue, Kristoffer. "AOC, Sanders Call for 'Climate Emergency' Declaration in Congress." inside climate news, July 10, 2019. Accessed August 8, 2019. http://insideclimatenews.org/news/09072019/sanders-aoc-ocasio-cortez-climate-change-emergency-declaration-congress-washington-flooding.

"Ekemini Uwan Interview by Elizabeth Woodson." (May 2019). Accessed December 6, 2019. https://t.co/fgVcDdDqDk.

Lukianoff, Greg, and Jonathan Haidt. *The Coddling of the American Mind: How Good Intentions and Bad Ideas Are Setting up a Generation for Failure.* New York City: Penguin Books, 2019.

McDowell, Josh, and Sean McDowell. *The Beauty of Intolerance: Setting a Generation Free to Know Truth & Love.* Uhrichsville, Ohio: Shiloh Run Press, an imprint of Barbour Publishing,, 2016.

"Naturalism." *Merriam-Webster Dictionary*, Accessed December 9, 2019. https://www.merriam-webster.com/dictionary/ad%20hominem.

"Naturalism." *Merriam-Webster Dictionary*, Accessed December 9, 2019. http://www.merriam-webster.com/dictionary/naturalism.

Pearcey, Nancy R. *Love Thy Body: Answering Hard Questions About Life and Sexuality*. Grand Rapids: Baker Books, 2018.

Delgado, Richard, and Jean Stefancic. *Critical race theory: An Introduction*. New York: New York University Press, 2001.

Nell Irvin Painter. "What Is Whiteness?" *The New York Times* (June 20, 2015). Accessed December 6, 2019. https://www.nytimes.com/2015/06/21/opinion/sunday/what-is-whiteness.html.

Thomas, Rob, Paul Doucette, Kyle Cook, and Brian Yale. *How Far We've Come*. N.p.: Sony/ATV Music Publishing LLC, 2007.

McDowell, Josh. *The Beauty of Intolerance: Setting a Generation Free to Know Truth & Love*. Uhrichsville, Ohio: Shiloh Run Press, an imprint of Barbour Publishing,, 2016.

McIntosh, P. "White Privilege: Unpacking the Invisible Knapsack." *Peace and Freedom* (July/August 1989): 10–12.

Novak, Michael. "Defining Social Justice." *First Things* (December 2000): 10–12. Accessed November 18, 2019. http://www.firstthings.com/article/2000/12/defining-social-justice.

Packer, J. I. *Knowing God*. Downers Grove, Ill: InterVarsity Press, 1973.

Palmer, Geraldine L. "People Who Are Homeless Are "People" First: Opportunity for Community Psychologist to Lead Through Language Reframing." *Global Journal of Community Psychology Practice* 9, no. 2 (November 2018). Accessed November

6,   2019.
https://www.gjcpp.org/en/article.php?issue=30&article=180.

———. "People Who Are Homeless Are "People" First: Opportunity for Community Psychologist to Lead Through Language Reframing." *Global Journal of Community Psychology Practice* 9, no. 2 (November 2018). Accessed November 6, 2019. https://www.gjcpp.org/en/article.php?issue=30&article=180.

———. "People Who Are Homeless Are "People" First: Opportunity for Community Psychologist to Lead Through Language Reframing." *Global Journal of Community Psychology Practice* 9, no. 2 (November 2018). Accessed November 6, 2019. https://www.gjcpp.org/en/article.php?issue=30&article=180.

———. "People Who Are Homeless Are "People" First: Opportunity for Community Psychologist to Lead Through Language Reframing." *Global Journal of Community Psychology Practice* 9, no. 2 (November 2018). Accessed November 6, 2019. https://www.gjcpp.org/en/article.php?issue=30&article=180.

———. "People Who Are Homeless Are "People" First: Opportunity for Community Psychologist to Lead Through Language Reframing." *Global Journal of Community Psychology Practice* 9, no. 2 (November 2018). Accessed November 6, 2019. https://www.gjcpp.org/en/article.php?issue=30&article=180.

Patricia Hill Collins, and Sirma Bilge. *Intersectionality*. 2nd ed. Key concepts. Medford, MA: Polity Press, 2020.

racism. *Oxford Advanced Learner's Dictionary*. 8th ed. N.p.: Oxford University Press, 2013.

Rauch, Jonathan. "Speaking as A..." *The New York Review of Books* 64, no. 17 (November 2017): 10–13.

"Virtue Signaling." Accessed October 22, 2019. http://dictionary.cambridge.org/us/dictionary/english/virtue-signalling.

"Trojan Horse (n.)." *The Merriam-Webster.com Dictionary*, https://www.merriam-webster.com/dictionary/Trojan%20horse.

Whitcomb, J.A. "Conceptions of Teacher Education." In *International Encyclopedia of Education*, edited by Penelope Peterson, Eva Baker, and Barry McGaw. Third Edition ed., 598–603. Oxford: Elsevier, 2010.

About the Author

Walter Swaim was born and raised in Miami, Florida. Though growing up in church most of his life, it was at his first summer youth camp in 1979 he responded to the Good News of Jesus Christ by receiving Him as his Lord and Savior. From that moment on, his life was changed forever. Though he originally had plans to do otherwise Walter sensed a deep desire, a calling, to go into vocational ministry and obeyed that call.

While attending Baptist Bible College in Springfield, Missouri he sensed God's direction to be a missionary in Argentina and shortly afterward married the love of his life. For over 34 years, he and his wife have served in ministry as missionaries and church planters in

Argentina and Florida, and now pastoring in Texas. Walter also serves a chaplain for local police and for corporations. He has attained both a M.Div. and Ph.D. from Louisiana Baptist Theological Seminary, concentrating his studies in apologetics.

He and his wife of 34 years reside in the Houston area and have 3 grown children and several grandchildren. Walt loves enjoying time with his family, fishing, reading, seeing historic sites, the occasional video game, and is a radio hobbyist as well. His favorite Scriptures are John 15:4-5 where Christ simply said, "Abide in Me."